*And

My Summer Sabbatical:

Cycling Across Switzerland and France

Via The Alps, Jura, Vosges & Champagne

My Summer Sabbatical:
Cycling Across Switzerland and France

By Andi Lonnen

© Andi Lonnen 2013

The right of Andi Lonnen to be identified as the author of this work has been asserted in accordance with Section 77 of the Copyright, Designs and Patents Act 1988.

No part of this book may be reproduced or distributed in any form or by any means, electronic or mechanical, or stored in a database or retrieval system, without prior written consent from the author.

To all my family, friends & kind strangers en route who supported me so wonderfully whilst I was on tour and most especially to my amazing Mum and to my fabulous sister, Jan

Chapter 1: The Inspiration

Ever since reading Enid Blyton's Famous Five and Secret Seven books, I'd always wanted to have "adventures". Maybe I didn't want to get in as many scrapes as they did, but I loved the idea of being outdoors as much as possible, exploring new places and having lots and lots of picnics!

Cycling and cycle touring have been a passion and way of life for me for many years now. After dipping my toes into the odd cycling weekend away in the UK and an organised week-long cycling tour from Barcelona to the Mediterranean in Spain (mostly all downhill), my first "proper" tour was from Land's End to John O'Groats with my Dad in June 2007. This was either going to make or break my desire for cycle touring adventures. Fortunately, despite cycling through the wettest June on record (until 2012), I was hooked!

This trip was an organised one. The cycle touring company, Bike Adventures, planned the route, organised the overnight accommodation, carried the luggage, assisted with any mechanical issues or breakdowns and, best of all, provided an awesome afternoon tea every day! So this was quite a "soft landing" into the world of cycle touring. It's an excellent way to find out if you enjoy it; you meet and cycle with a group of like-minded people often making lifelong friends along the way and it takes all the time and hassle out of planning trips when you have a busy job and life.

A number of other organised tours with the same company followed including a week in Corsica (I got the onset of hypothermia in appalling conditions in the mountains along with two other chaps and we were rescued by the support van – another advantage to group organised trips), a 2 week trip cycling the length of France from the English Channel to the Mediterranean coast and, after plucking up the confidence, I then tackled the 10 day "Raid Pyrenean" which climbs 28 mountain cols from the Mediterranean to the Atlantic across the stunning Pyrenees and this was followed a year later by cycling many of the cols in the French Alps made famous by the Tour de France for 2 weeks. My heart is always happiest in the mountains. I had initially been reluctant to cycle there with a group, thinking I would be with mega-athletes and would hold everyone up. Nothing could have been further from the truth.

Most of us chugged up the mountains at the pace of a tortoise, chatting away and with as many tea and pastry stops as possible. It is the only way to cycle tour!

Bike Adventures offered the option of hotel accommodation or camping trips. I'd always opted for the hotel accommodation claiming the need for a warm room, a comfortable bed and an en-suite was paramount after a day on the saddle in all weathers. And sometimes the thought of the hotel room was the only thing to get me through a tough day on the bike. However, if I wanted to go on the Pyrenees trip, the only option that year was camping. Hmmm.

I eventually caved and agreed to the camping holiday. I hired a tent and sleeping bag from Bike Adventures and, although I was looking forward to the actual cycling, I was dreading the whole camping experience.

Well, I fell in love with it and have never looked back since! I love how cosy camping is and it's much warmer and more comfortable than you imagine. On the Pyrenees tour, we experienced everything from temperatures soaring towards the 40s on the Mediterranean coast to violent thunderstorms in the mountains. I was shaking like a leaf the first night I was camping in a thunderstorm but then I realised the next morning that (a) we were all still alive and (b) most people had snored their way through it anyway so if they weren't bothered then I clearly didn't need to be. So the mixed weather didn't put me off. In fact the bad weather made it feel more exciting and adventurous! And, overall, I enjoyed the increased sociability that camping offers above hotel trips.

Every holiday thereafter would need to be camping now, it was the only way forward for me. I researched and bought a lightweight, storm-proof tent as well as all the necessary camping equipment, which I then tested on the French Alps trip the following year. The weather for that two weeks was absolutely dreadful and likely to put off even the hardiest campers for life. Although it was admittedly very difficult to keep anything dry, I still adored camping. I loved the camaraderie and spirit of the other cycle campers in our group. We kept each other going, and I loved the sanctuary and cosiness that my tent provided. Bad weather camping was really the main experience I'd had by that stage and I thought good weather camping must indeed be very dull!

Most of my tours by this stage had been organised and with a luggage transfer service. What would it be like to carry all my camping gear on my touring bike and try a solo tour? How would I devise my own route when all routes had been organised for me previously. Given my proximity to the stunning Yorkshire Dales, I took my first tentative steps into solo cycle-camping one August Bank Holiday weekend. I didn't tell many people in case I couldn't do it! What was I worried about? It was wonderful! The sense of adventure and achievement in carrying my own home up and down through the Yorkshire Dales and the self-sufficiency was excellent. And, again, it was incredibly sociable to say I was on my own. Cycling on a fully laden touring bike invites lots of questions from curious customers in tea-shops and at campsites and even if you just pull off and stop somewhere to admire the view. I find it thoroughly enjoyable engaging with so many different people.

As many cycle-camping weekends away as possible followed and I spent the Winter planning my first solo cycle-camping tour in Europe for the following Summer. Whilst researching which country to visit, using the eurovelo network as a starting point (many thanks to Otley cycle club rider John Bennett for that tip!), I was really surprised to learn that Switzerland was a country with an extensive cycling network. Having visited Switzerland a number of times in the Winter months to cross country ski, I thought it would be a stunningly beautiful place to cycle in the Summer. I also felt very safe there. Much of my research was carried out on the www.veloland.ch website (information is provided in English). There are 9 national cycle routes and I chose Route 4 Alpine Panorama, given my love of the mountains. This was a route from St Margrethen in the east of the country close to the Austrian border and then via the Swiss Alps to Aigle in the south west, not far from Geneva. This gave me the additional bonus of being able to visit my friend, Mary, who lives near Geneva, at the end of the tour. She had just had her first baby, a little boy called Maxime, and I couldn't wait to meet him!

Given this was my Summer holiday and would involve 2 weeks away from my busy job, I contacted a company called Swiss

Trails. They organised all the campsites for me and I arranged luggage transfer through them as well for a surprisingly reasonable price given Switzerland is such an expensive country. This took a lot of pressure off and saved me a considerable amount of time. Again, it was a bit of a soft landing for my first solo tour abroad. I must admit that I didn't know Switzerland was big on campsites, I thought they would be too much of a blot on their picture-perfect scenery!

As Winter progressed into Spring, it became clear that my new job wasn't what I'd hoped it would be and I decided to leave. I had a 3 month notice period to work which conveniently took me up to the start date of my Swiss holiday. During this notice period, I suddenly thought, why not extend my Summer holiday by another day or so and I could then spend more time with Mary and Maxime. Now that I had the time, I realised I could also spend some more time cycling in the region. Another "day or so" became a week, which then became a month. It was too good an opportunity to miss. I had no idea where exactly I wanted to spend this extra month cycling so I had an exciting few weeks exploring all the options.

I also decided this would be the perfect early 40th birthday present to myself. My birthday is in the depths of Winter which is not conducive to a cycle-camping tour. I couldn't think of a better way to celebrate my 40th.

And so my first solo cycle-camping tour overseas was born!

Chapter 2 – Questions and Concerns

"It's not safe to cycle on your own, is it?" "What do you do if your bike breaks down?" "Don't you get lonely on your own?" "Wow, you must be super-fit to do a cycle tour, mustn't you?" I am asked these and many other questions all the time. I therefore hope to address some of these in this chapter and throughout the book to help dispel some myths and fears.

Firstly, many female cyclists (men, too!) are concerned about maintaining and repairing the bike en route. Given I would be touring for at least 3 times longer than usual, I knew I needed to be as competent as possible at looking after my bike and being able to mend it in case of mechanical breakdown. I have taken part in a number of bike maintenance courses over the years. They are definitely worthwhile attending if you want to build such skills and they definitely boost your confidence. The only downside is if you don't get to practise and use the skills, it is easy to forget them. When I cycle with my local cycling club, those who are the most skilled mechanically tend to deal with any problems en route to ensure the club can get back on the road as quickly and efficiently as possible.

To keep the key skills fresh in my mind, I spent an afternoon with a friend from the club, Brian. I knew I could deal with punctures, albeit very slowly, so I wanted to spend time understanding issues that can arise with brakes, gears and the chain. Brian even brought a bit of chain with him so we could break and re-attach it. We also ran through daily checks I should carry out whilst on the road, such as checking the tyres for sufficient pressure and to ensure there were no glass or stones stuck in them, checking the brake blocks for wear, ensuring all fastenings were tight including bottle cages, the luggage rack and pannier fittings, etc.

This refresher session helped a great deal. I put the bike in for a service at my local bike shop around 6 weeks before the trip. I knew there would be bike shops en route in Switzerland and France, even if I had to hop on a train to get to the nearest big town. I just hoped nothing major would go wrong!

I always, always get asked if I get lonely. Never! In fact, it is sometimes difficult to escape from people! Cycling on a fully laden bike is a real conversation starter. So many people want to know what you are doing, where you have come from, where you are going, if you like their country, etc. My faith in humanity has been restored since I started cycle touring. People are often so willing to help, be it with directions, offering a towel to dry yourself and your bike after a rainstorm, giving you food or drink and they are generally very supportive with your endeavours. I've had people stop to check I'm OK and if I need anything after they've seen me at a café earlier in the day. I've had teenage boys applaud me as I summit a mountain col and then run over to give me an energy bar or a banana and a pat on the back. I've had people want me to go on television to show other potential female cycle tourers how amazing the world of cycle touring is!

With technology today, it is easier than ever to stay in touch with friends and family whilst on the road. This helps deal with any homesickness, knowing you have the support of loved ones back home. I wrote a blog en route, which could be written from my Blackberry, so everyone who wanted to could keep up to date with my progress. There had been over 4,000 hits from around the world by the time I returned to the UK!

I know from reading books by other cycle-tourers that evenings can be a problem for some. I don't think I have ever found this to be an issue. There is generally quite a bit to do after pitching camp for the evening, including showering, the laundry, checking and cleaning the bike, food shopping, cooking and eating, going for a wander around the village or town you are staying in, writing your diary, updating the blog, reading books on the Kindle, listening to music on the iPod. I can never stay up late at night anyway, I'm generally shattered from cycling in the fresh air all day and am happy to settle down to sleep between 9-10pm, depending on when it gets dark.

There are times when I wish people were with me so I could share a stunning view with them or a particularly delicious meal out. However, I can tell them all about it on the blog and they can respond. I know they are with me in spirit and that keeps me going.

"It isn't safe for a woman to cycle on her own" is an apparent statement of fact I hear a lot. Nonsense! Refer back to what I said earlier about the kindness, support and encouragement I receive from people on the road. Yes, there may be the odd one who ruins it for everyone. However, you can't live your life thinking about the "odd one" otherwise you'd never do anything. There is a risk of having an accident every time you get into a car but we don't think of it like this given travelling by car is such a normal part of every day life for us. There are lots of books and blogs out there by women of all ages who have cycle toured on their own to the most remote places in the world. They are very inspiring.

I had chosen to cycle in civilised western countries where I had a working knowledge of the local language. I felt as safe and well looked after in these countries as my own. I was checking in every day by writing the blog. I was staying on established campsites with other people around. I had the telephone numbers of the emergency services for each country plugged into my phone.

Of course it is wise to stay alert and be aware when cycling and this goes for men as well as women. The biggest risk to cyclists is generally other traffic on the roads. I've found that vehicles give me plenty more room when they see all the panniers. I must look bigger than I really am! I do appreciate the extra care motorists take.

When I tell people about the tour, they exclaim I must be super fit. You definitely don't need to be super fit to cycle tour. The beauty of cycle touring is that it can be anything anyone wants it to be – slow and leisurely with minimum distances travelled every day or faster with a focus on mile munching. I'm somewhere in between with an appreciation for soaking up the scenery and atmosphere of everywhere I'm cycling through.

Something I rarely get asked but can be an issue for female tourers is finding somewhere to go to the loo! It was a real issue cycling across the Swiss Alps, in particular. Swiss chalets are placed just far enough from each other that there was nowhere to hide for a quick wee. The roads are often built into mountains and hills with sheer drops and are therefore not conducive for a quick run into the bushes. It was simply a case of grabbing any opportunity when it arose, keeping an eye out for a copse of trees or a wall to duck behind, making the most of any café stops and looking for public toilets in towns and villages. Public toilets in Switzerland are absolutely spotless.

All of these are infinitely preferable to the pain of cycling with a full bladder!

Chapter 3: What to take

How exciting, an extended tour to look forward to! Now, what would I need to pack for 6 weeks?

Having toured for many years, particularly in the mountains, I have now got my kit list down to a fine art. Here, I explain my thought process because I know it is an issue for everyone who tours, from a novice to an experienced tourer. This is what works for me personally, however everyone is different. Some will wish to carry more, some considerably less. This should help to provide a useful guideline. There is also a full kit list of everything I took on tour in the appendix at the back of this book.

Of paramount importance was keeping the amount I took and the weight I would be carrying down to an absolute minimum whilst also being able to enjoy some comforts. I knew I could experience all weathers, everything from freezing cold snowy mountains to torrential rain and thunderstorms to hot sunny weather in the valleys.

Because I tour quite regularly, I have a packing checklist template on my laptop which I can easily adapt depending on the length of tour I am doing and particularly on the weather conditions. Once updated, I print this checklist out and tick everything off as I pack it into my panniers. This may sound like I need to get out more! However, I love the planning and organising stage as much as the actual tour itself, so this bit is fun for me. More importantly, it does mean I have everything I need and nothing is forgotten, so it is worth doing.

I use the Ortlieb luggage system to carry all my kit. Ortlieb panniers are fully waterproof and well worth the investment particularly if you are touring in the often soggy UK or in the mountains. They are pretty indestructible, too. For this tour, given its longevity and the fact that I would be camping and cooking, I took two rear panniers, two front panniers, a rack pack and a handlebar bag. This provided excellent balance on the bike and all the space I needed to carry everything.

My tent and most sleeping equipment were stored in my rack pack, which sits on top of my rear panniers. I have a Vaude Taurus Ultralite tent, which weighs just under 2kg and is easy to carry in the rack pack or on top of the bike as the tent poles fold down to a convenient size. This tent is also very waterproof, has space to sit up in, which I find important after a day on the bike, and has a lovely little porch which fits all my panniers beautifully. I use a self-inflating sleeping mat and I invested in a good quality down sleeping bag from Alpkit a few years ago. It packs down so small and is very lightweight for carrying. Most importantly, it is blissful to snuggle down in and very toasty for sleeping in.

I was hugely enthusiastic about my new cooking kit! My good friend, Adele, had recommended a gas burning trangia. They heat really quickly and the heat is fully controllable. I therefore took my new and fabulous gas burning trangia with 1 saucepan, the frying pan that doubles as a lid and a cute and gorgeous tiny little kettle. Yes, I could have saved weight here but I wanted a robust, stable cooking system that was as storm-proof as possible to cook decent meals for several weeks. The kettle was an added luxury however, as my Grandad says, I am a real "tea-belly". I initially took 2 gas canisters with me and planned to buy more en route. From research, however, I knew that these screw-top canisters were almost impossible to buy in France other than in Decathlon stores in major towns and cities, the likes of which I didn't plan to cycle through. Therefore, I also took a meths burner with me. I knew I could buy meths or another suitable liquid if needed. The meths burner is only small and does not weigh much.

Although I appreciate you can use plastic carrier bags to pack clothes and other bit and pieces, I use the Eagle Creek packing system of "cubes", whether I'm cycle touring, visiting family or friends for the weekend or if I'm travelling on business. They keep everything well organised, are slimline and easy to pack, they weigh almost nothing and they come in different designs and colours so I easily know what bit of kit is kept in which cube. I keep my cycling kit in one cube, my evening clothes in another and my other bits and pieces in another. I did say I like being organised! It keeps everything in order in the tent and avoids the usual "pannier explosion" when tipping out your bags.

With regards to clothing, both on and off the bike, I needed layers to deal with all weathers and items that could wash and dry quickly. Being girlie, everything had to match as much as possible! I then felt that I had an extensive wardrobe with many different clothing combinations.

I was very impressed with myself for managing to whittle down the number of toiletries I normally take and consider essential. However, my good buddy Teresa, the queen of lightweight travel, was shocked at how much I was still planning to take. (I was relieved she hadn't seen the travel hairdryer and hair straighteners that I'd tried to pack earlier!) She was right. I learnt en route that shampoo, for example, can be used for more than just hair washing; I used it as my shower gel and laundry wash, too. But I refused to part with my miniature bottle of lavender oil. It helps me relax and sleep, makes my tent smell lovely and it is fantastic to massage into sore muscles and, in my case, an arthritic neck, to alleviate any aches and pains. It is important for me to feel and smell clean and nice in the evenings after cycling so the extra weight of some "luxury" toiletries is worth it for me personally.

I really appreciated Teresa's ruthless approach to my packing and I did expel a number of items from the panniers. I know I was grateful not to have the extra weight whilst battling up mountain cols carrying this little lot. The critical eye of a friend can really help ascertain what is truly essential.

Every cycle-tourer has at least one luxury item they take with them on tour. This can be something like a book or a cuddly toy. I take several luxury items! My key piece of luxury kit was my Thermarest chair, which converted my sleeping mat into a chair. Oh, the bliss! It is an exceptionally lightweight piece of kit and still one of the best things I have ever bought for camping tours.

Other items I couldn't have lived without on tour included my Blackberry, essential to keep in touch with everyone back home via text, email and, occasionally, phone as well as to take photos and update my blog; my Kindle, whereby I had already downloaded a number of cycle touring books for inspiration en route; and my iPod, which is barely the size of a postage stamp. And I always take a notebook and pen to keep a diary every day. I love reading about and re-living my adventures and exploits, particularly in the dark Winter months. And you never know when you're going to need your diary to write a book!

Chapter 4: Getting there and back

The thought of travelling with a bike and considerable number of panniers from the UK to the other side of Switzerland was probably more daunting than the few weeks of cycling I had planned.

I undertook lots of research – seriously, what did we do before Google and the internet? I looked into trains, ferries, planes and the European Bike Express, a coach that carries bikes and luggage. The Man in Seat Sixty-One (www.seat61.com) was a particularly useful website.

I eventually decided on taking the train from my home in Yorkshire to the other side of Switzerland and then getting the European Bike Express back to the UK from Calais. For future trips, I wanted to know the benefits of both modes of transport. I was clear I did not want to take my touring bike by air. With 2 rear panniers, 2 front panniers, a rack pack containing my tent, etc., and a handlebar bag, can you imagine the baggage charges alone?! I was also adamant I didn't want to dismantle the bike on any part of the journey.

I was my usual organised self and booked all trains the very second tickets were available, generally 3 months in advance although I was able to book Eurostar 4 months in advance. This really keeps the costs of train travel to an absolute minimum and I wanted to ensure my bike was booked onto all relevant services at the earliest opportunity.

For those of you as daunted as I was about both the booking process and the actual travelling bit itself, it really isn't as scary as I thought and the process was not too complicated. I needed to pre-book the bike on the Intercity train from Leeds to London, the Eurostar from London to Paris and the fast train from Paris to Zurich. The Intercity East Coast train I could book easily and quickly online, this included booking my bike onto the train. My bike even had it's very own ticket for travel in the train carriage.

With Eurostar, I firstly called them to ask if there were bike places available on the train I wished to travel on. Once confirmed, I booked my seat online and then called them back to book my bike onto the same service as me. You need to have your seat reservation before you can book your bike onto the service. There is a cost to this, however I was happy that the bike was on the same train as me and I didn't need to dismantle it. You can dismantle and bag your bike up so it can travel with you as part of your normal luggage for no additional cost or you can also send your bike as registered baggage for a fee, although this does not guarantee your bike will be on the same train as you. However it is guaranteed to arrive 24 hours after registration so you could send your bike the day before and then collect it on arrival in Paris.

For the Paris to Zurich leg, I contacted Rail Europe by telephone and they were very helpful and friendly. They advised I didn't need to pre-book on the local trains after Zurich, although I would personally do this in future. Buying tickets in a major city station whilst keeping your bike and luggage with you at all times on your own is quite tricky, so having the tickets immediately to hand would have definitely been much easier.

Booking on the European Bike Express was very straightforward and simple. This can be done online via their website. I needed to change the date and pick-up location from my original booking, given I was now cycling for another month and, again, this was very easy to do. The service was always friendly and helpful. I was really looking forward to trying out the bike bus and meeting lots of other cycle-tourers. The bikes are carried in a trailer at the back. You just need to turn your handlebars before they can load the bikes on which is definitely within anyone's capabilities (including mine!).

You'll read throughout this book that travelling with the bike and luggage was quite straightforward and definitely nothing to be feared. There are always wonderful people around to help where needed. I wouldn't hesitate to take my bike on trains and on the bike bus in the future.

Chapter 5 – Wednesday 18th July 2012: From Ilkley to Paris by Train

Wow, here we go! After all these weeks of planning and packing, my dream was finally becoming a reality.

I actually slept surprisingly well the night before setting off, which was quite unexpected. Usually my mind is whizzing around with everything I may or may not have forgotten and what may or may not go wrong. However, I'd had a couple of calm days packing, unpacking and re-packing so I felt well prepared and knew everything fitted comfortably into my panniers. Lightweight travellers would be horrified at the amount I was taking but I was confident my luxury items would be worth the extra weight for the comfort they would provide over the next few weeks. And, by luxury, I mean having two t-shirts instead of one and a fleece bodywarmer rather than doing without!

I was still a little apprehensive at the next two days of travel and prepared myself to exercise unusual levels of patience where needed.

This first day was my shortest and easiest cycling day of the trip, freewheeling for approximately 100 yards downhill to my local railway station! As my bike and I boarded the train, a chap came running over to ask if I was cycling the Way of the Roses, a fabulous cycling route from Morecambe on the west coast of the UK to Bridlington on the east coast. I explained that no, I was heading to Europe however I had cycled the Way of the Roses so we had a quick natter about that. He wished me luck for my forthcoming trip.

At Leeds City station, another guy on a bike came up for a chat about what I was doing and where I was going. He was actually just returning from three days cycling the southern loop of the Lancashire Cycle Way. I asked where his luggage was and he said this was everything – he had a tiny rear bag and that was all! I carry more on a Sunday club ride!

I'd never travelled with my bike on an InterCity train however there was no need to be concerned. The guard showed me to the relevant part of the train and helped me heave my bike on board. I could leave the panniers on given no people were allowed in this area so I simply took my handlebar bag with me to my seat. Normally I listen to my iPod or read my Kindle or a magazine whilst travelling to pass the time but my head was busy enough and the journey flew.

At King's Cross, the guard's van had been opened and, as I was lifting my bike down, a wonderful railway worker appeared seemingly from nowhere to help me. This became a feature of the trip – someone always seemed to appear when you most needed them. Fabulous!

Fortunately, I only had to wheel the bike around the corner to St Pancras station. With a little help, I found the Euro Despatch area where I needed to take my bike to travel on the Eurostar. It was basically in the coach park (obviously?!). Again, the process was so straightforward. After simply showing my booking invoice, all I had to do was remove the panniers and they wheeled the bike away from me to load onto my train a short while later. Now the tricky part: trying to carry 2 rear panniers, 2 front panniers, a rack pack and a handle bar bag….

I shuffled along in a not very dignified but otherwise successful manner to the closest café, arranged all the bags as best I could around a table and ordered a much-needed cuppa. My lovely sister, Jan, would soon be arriving and travelling to Paris with me. When she heard this had become an early 40th birthday present to myself, she definitely wanted to join in. I was hugely excited that she would be coming along. We live hundreds of miles away from each other and rarely get to meet up. This was therefore a great opportunity. I was also suddenly realising what an enormous help she would be with all my luggage!

Once reunited, it was all chatter and giggles as we caught up on each other's lives and our forthcoming overnight trip to Paris. Chris, a good friend of Jan and her partner, Gus, lives in Paris and he was meeting us at the Gare du Nord station. Jan was looking forward to seeing him again, I was looking forward to meeting him. I'd heard lots about him. I had been slightly concerned that he would make me do some push-ups or something, which apparently they all did when they got together being fitness freaks! I like gently and quietly pedalling on my bicycle, not doing anything as hard core as push ups!

The day had run so beautifully smoothly so far. It was alas not to last. As we went through security at Eurostar with all my many bags, I was pulled to one side and my painstakingly carefully packed panniers were emptied onto their counters. I wondered what they were after. It is possible to even take firearms on board Eurostar!

Horror of horrors, they confiscated my precious gas canisters, the source of my tea making and cooking evening meals. "But how will I make my cups of tea?" I wailed. Whilst this was met with both surprising sympathy and understandable amusement by Eurostar officials (and complete embarrassment by my sister), the answer remained a firm "no, Madame, you cannot take these gas canisters on board". It was little consolation that the officials praised my first class packing skills in an attempt to cheer me up.

Jan was straight on the phone to Chris in Paris. He was actually in a meeting at work so was attempting to surreptitiously communicate with us. He knew of a Decathlon store in Paris but it would close at 7pm. This wouldn't give us much time after we arrived.

Chris was well up for the challenge! He was waiting for us outside the Gare du Nord in Paris with his shiny new motorbike. After an enthusiastic reunion between him and Jan and introductions for me, I rapidly explained exactly what I needed and, with a big rev of his engine and an impressive wheelie, Chris zoomed off on a mad dash across Paris with only 20 minutes before Decathlon closed. His mission was a success with several small replacement canisters purchased. He is now known to me as Hero Chris of the Gas Canister Saga!

In the meantime, I had located Euro Despatch at the station to collect my bike. There she was, gleaming and happily waiting for me, fully in tact and ready for the adventures ahead.

My sister and I walked together around 3 miles across Paris from the Gare du Nord to near the Gare de Lyon, where I would be catching my train the following morning. After checking in at our hotel for the night and securely locking my bike in the hotel's garage, Chris joined us both for a delicious dinner. We had a very lively evening catching up on all the gossip as well as laughing with relief about the events of the last few hours. Being treated as a potential bombmaker at the Eurostar terminal had certainly added some excitement and spice to the journey so far!

Chapter 6 – Thursday 19th July 2012: From Paris to St Margrethen by Train

Day one of travelling had been mostly relaxing and generally enjoyable and I was hoping for a calm and easy second day of travelling. It would also be preferable not to be treated as a potential bomb-maker if I could help it.

My sister had to leave by 6.30am as she was heading back to work in London that day. She had treated herself to a first class Eurostar ticket back, which included a posh breakfast, much needed for her long day ahead.

I ambled down to breakfast at the hotel a short while later where my eyes lit up at all the juices, fruit, cereals, yoghurts, pastries and, yes, they had a plethora of different teas to try, excellent! The signs above the food were a little unusual; cereal was described as "fibre", milk and yoghurts had "calcium" written by them and so on. I suppose it helps promote a healthy diet.

Although I was only about one minute's walk from Gare de Lyon where I was catching my train to Zurich, anyone who knows me will tell you I like to be hyper-early for anything, particularly public transport. I wanted to get everything loaded onto the bike and be at the station in very good time. It took me a couple of goes to get all the bags down to the garage and then a further few minutes to unlock and load up the bike. With a mixture of French and English, the guy on reception told me to simply press the button to let myself out of the garage rather than him doing it from reception whilst he was busy checking out lots of people. That sounded easy enough.

Except I apparently pressed the wrong button. Oh! He didn't say there was more than one button and the one I pressed was right by the garage door. It apparently had a notice some distance away in French saying under no circumstances should anyone push this button. Why put it by the garage door then?! Cover it up in a locked frame away from the likes of me! The guy came running down from Reception, now unable to open the garage door from upstairs and he couldn't seem to open it manually either. Why on earth would you have a button that you shouldn't press right by the garage door, especially one that then completely locks and traps you in the garage? The actual button I should have pressed was somewhere around the corner. It was starting to feel like something from Father Ted.

After a lot of banging and pulling of various strings and levers, the annoyed Frenchman let a rather agitated me escape to the outside world. 20 minutes had passed. I sprinted to the station. I'd been to Gare de Lyon before and remember getting completely lost in there so wanted plenty of time to find where I needed to be. I can't imagine why I got lost in there previously; it was thankfully so easy to find both the platform I needed and then the platform itself. Needing to calm my jangled nerves, I inevitably headed straight for a relaxing cuppa and started to chuckle at this morning's shenanigans. My sense of humour was intact. What mattered was I was here now and in good time.

Looking at the departure board, I frowned as I tried to remember what "retarde" meant. What on earth was a retarded train? A tardy train...oh my goodness, my train was late! After all that effort! Weren't trains always on time in France and Switzerland?

I discovered from the travel information desk that the train was 40 minutes late. I didn't have specific trains to catch after Zurich and I should still make it comfortably to St Margrethen near the Austrian border before dark. So thankfully it wasn't a big deal.

As we boarded our late train, we were all handed a box of food and drink goodies. I've no idea if this is normal practise or simply because the train was delayed. There were some quite nice things in this box especially the pureed fruit compote. They are not easily found in the UK (outside of baby food sections anyway!) but they are everywhere in Switzerland and France and I absolutely adore them. Almost as much as tea! I happily swapped my crisps for fruit compotes from other travellers. Yummy!

On this train from Paris to Zurich, my designated seat was in the bicycle carriage allowing me to remain with my bike, which I thought was an excellent idea. The guard had unfortunately sent me running to the wrong end of the lengthy train so, when I ran back to where I started, I was the last one on with my bike. It is pretty tricky to get your bike and bags onto these trains however there are usually plenty of people to help. It made me realise that we are lucky that some of our local trains in the UK are easy to wheel a bike (or pram or wheelchair) straight on with their wide doors and easy access from the platform.

The journey passed uneventfully and I arrived in Zurich early afternoon. Although Zurich was the end of the line, people were already trying to get on the train as I was trying to get off. With the narrow door and steep steps, my only option was to run down the steps with two panniers, run back on and off the train with another two, run back on and off with the final two and then run back on and off the train with my bike. As with all experiences on this trip, there were some super people who did everything to help me, whilst others sadly were trying to knock me over in their rush to get on the train. There were some cyclists on the platform who pulled my bags to one side and stood guard to keep them safe and they also helped me get my bike down. It is manageable on your own, I say this as a fairly weedy female cyclist, however, it is so much nicer when warm, kind and friendly strangers do everything to assist. I always ensure I do the same for others, it makes such a difference.

As mentioned earlier, it would have been much easier if I'd had flexible tickets pre-booked for my next two trains. Instead, I took my bike into the ticket office with me, not wanting to leave it outside with my entire home on it. I know it was a bit in the way and I apologise to those who had to put up with that. There was some confusion over which trains I could catch and whether my bike needed to be pre-booked, however the supervisor was able to help and I eventually got the tickets I needed. It costs a child's fare to take a bike on a train in Switzerland. It was a bit pricey but it would get me to my starting point.

The first of these two trains was really busy in the bike carriage and reservations were not needed. Fortunately, I got my bike and me on safely, however other cyclists were not able to get on and had to wait for the next train. I was really relieved. Again, you were able to sit comfortably with your bike in the bike carriage.

I nearly missed the next train although there would have been another one in 30 minutes. This train had such steep steps and the guard was frantically blowing the whistle if I wanted to get on. I managed to throw the panniers onto the train but the guard wouldn't help me get the bike on, which was simply not possible in this case on my own. So, who came to the rescue? A little old lady who had been watching from inside the carriage. Bless her! She was certainly very sprightly and seemingly had no difficulty hoisting my heavy touring bike up as I pushed from below.

What a relief to finally reach St Margrethen after two full days of travelling, being treated as a suspected bomb-maker in London, being locked in an underground garage in Paris after pressing the wrong button and after lugging my bike and six pieces of luggage on and off six different trains in the UK, France and Switzerland.

I reached the campsite in St Margrethen in the early evening. It was an absolute joy to finally put my tent up and feel like my cycle tour was truly about to start. The fresh air, the sweet smell of the grass and the birds singing all added to my happiness. I was able to stretch my legs and take a stroll around the campsite which had a large swimming pool and a lovely lake. The campsite were expecting me and gave me a large pack put together by Swiss Trails. This had everything I needed for my Alpine Panorama tour across Switzerland. What a welcome!

Much as I wanted to test my hard-won gas canisters and cook on the trangia, there was no fresh food on site to cook with, however there were a number of eating places. Burgers and sausages appeared to dominate the menus in the café and restaurant, which didn't help me as a vegetarian. Fortunately they also offered a simple, and delicious, cheese and tomato pizza which I enjoyed with a fresh green salad and a chilled glass of dry white wine. The pizza was enormous! I'd forgotten the portion sizes in Switzerland which accompany the high prices. Salads are invariably drowned in a rather tasty zingy mayonnaise. A mint tea and an early night followed. As I drifted off to sleep, as a sufferer of motion sickness, I still felt like I was going up and down on the trains. Weird!

Chapter 7 – Friday 20th July 2012: Cycling from St Margrethen to Bachli

What an incredible night's sleep I had. I nearly always sleep so, so well in my tent. I was making up for the lack of sleep at the hotel in Paris and the relief at having completed those 2 days of travelling ensured a night of blissful deep sleep. I'd been more concerned about those two days of travelling than I was about the forthcoming several weeks of cycling.

I was up and about early, indulging in a big bowl of Weetabix and sultanas with some lovely creamy Swiss milk and, you guessed it, a steaming mug of tea. Although it was a cloudy morning, it was warm enough to wear shorts and a t-shirt, something we don't seem to have been able to do in the UK for many Summers.

I'm rather baffled to say it took me two hours to get myself ready, eat breakfast, take the tent down, pack everything up and load it onto the bike. I knew I would get quicker as the tour progressed. I like to set off at a reasonable time in the morning, and certainly by 9am, otherwise I feel behind all day.

I'd arranged luggage transfer with Swiss Trails, however this only covered 1 set of panniers otherwise the costs would increase substantially. I therefore left my rear panniers at reception for Swiss Trails to collect and cycled carrying my rack pack, 2 front panniers and my handlebar bag, which usefully has a mapcase on it.

The Swiss cycle network is, as you would imagine, incredibly well organised with plentiful signposts. All I had to do was follow the number 4 sign and I would get from one side of their country to the other via the Swiss Alps. I thought the Velo Suisse map would have been included as part of the Swiss Trails pack, however it wasn't. I would need to look out for that en route as I don't like being without a map. Apparently you can buy them beforehand in the UK, it was simply that I didn't think I needed to buy one. In the pack, there was a book with reasonable maps in. At the moment, you can only get this book in French or German. My French is better than my German but by no means perfect so I couldn't follow much of the history and culture of the route. However, I could experience it as I pedalled.

The first stage of the ride was very straightforward following the number 4 signs through the sprawling industrial estate and towards the hills. Although these early hill climbs were much steeper than I'd imagined, the rolling and green Swiss scenery was certainly pretty despite this particular area being quite built up and busy. It is worth noting that sometimes the number 4 signs are replaced by a generic brown diamond sign with a picture of a cyclist. I soon learnt it was absolutely fine to follow these. They were more prevalent where a number of cycle routes converged.

I was lucky to find an excellent bakery and grocery store this morning where I stocked up on some fresh bread rolls, Swiss cheese, some fruit and a naughty chocolate croissant, essential soul food. There were water fountains everywhere I pedalled, so topping up with cool, fresh water was clearly not going to be an issue.

The sun did keep trying to make an appearance today but wasn't overly successful. In fact, much to my dismay, it started to rain in the afternoon and the temperature really dropped. I popped into a café for a hot chocolate to warm up and did my best to explain in German what I was doing. I can manage to order food and drink in cafes in German and can ask for and generally understand directions but I otherwise start to struggle. Fortunately, one of the owners spoke a little English and, between the two of us, I was able to get my story out and show the route in the book. They were impressed and this lifted my rainy mood.

I cycled 43 miles today. The route was very hilly, I was carrying a lot of weight on the bike therefore it took me all day to complete. My average speed was less than 8mph! This meant that unfortunately I didn't have time to explore the incredibly pretty town of Appelzell en route, although I felt privileged to cycle through such an outstandingly beautiful place. The Swiss certainly know how to do pretty. This felt such a shame. The purpose of touring on my own was to explore more than I otherwise would on a group tour. However, the Swiss element of my tour was all pre-booked and I needed to reach my next campsite in good time. I certainly didn't want to be arriving and putting my tent up in the dark.

I was able to buy a few provisions for the evening at a Co-op supermarket before reaching the campsite. Be aware! You need to weigh and label all fruit and vegetables yourself before going to the checkout. I didn't know this and then spent far too long enduring the sighs, tuts, shrugs and eye rolling of the teenager working on the till. Come on lad, it wasn't the end of the world!

By the time I arrived at my campsite in Bachli, it was raining cats and dogs, was freezing cold and it was so foggy, you could barely see your hand in front of you. Nearly all my cycle tours have been carried out in similarly atrocious weather and I was really hoping my luck would change on this one. Apparently not!

Swiss Trails had delivered my rear panniers in good time and they were waiting for me in reception. I then put the tent up as quickly as I could in the pouring rain. Tent poles are really slippery when wet! The activity was at least helping to keep me warm.

I was staying at a small but perfectly formed campsite with some really well thought through facilities including, can you believe it, a drying room. I guess it must rain there a lot. The indoor space was well heated and included a self-catering kitchen, a large dining room and a large lounge area along with the shower and bathroom facilities. Everything was so clean. Unlike France, Swiss campsites all seem to have toilet roll and soap too, such luxury!

I dashed indoors for a shower and life became truly great again. Ah, the power of a hot, steaming shower! They had even provided a hairdryer! I was now transformed from a shivering, bedraggled wreck into a warm, dry, clean, nice-smelling human being again.

Completely used to such dreadful weather conditions, I take a separate set of full waterproofs with me when camping to ensure my evening clothes never get wet. Lightweight cycle-campers would balk at me taking separate waterproofs to my cycling waterproofs. However, from past experience, I find it so unpleasant putting on smelly, wet waterproofs that I've cycled in during the day on top of my clean evening clothes.

This separate set of waterproofs would be considered yet another of my growing list of luxury items.

Although there was a (warm) self-catering kitchen, I wasn't sure my camp cooking pots and pans would survive on their hob. There was a sheltered area outside where I could cook and remain protected from the elements and therefore chose to set my little kitchen up here. I appreciate it's not very ambitious or imaginative to have pasta in tomato sauce when camping, however I couldn't think of anything tastier or more warming at that moment in time. I chopped and added a fresh carrot and courgette and subsequently enjoyed a truly delicious meal which thoroughly warmed me up. This was followed by my super-sized mug of hot tea. Even my toes were toasty by the time I'd finished.

After washing up and packing away, I snuggled down in my lovely tent and gorgeous sleeping bag with the rain lashing down outside. I don't know exactly why, but I do love being in the tent in torrential rain. I feel very safe and cosy. It's not much fun packing it up sopping wet in the morning but I would deal with that later. For now, I fell peacefully asleep as the rain continued to drum down on the tent.

Chapter 8 – Saturday 21st July 2012: Cycling from Bachli to Klontal

Although still very wet, cold and soggy when I woke up this morning and squelched my way to the shower block, some of the fog had started to lift, revealing a hint of what must be outstanding views. I was surprised to realise how high up we were.

I was so hungry and tucked into a hearty breakfast. At least the milk had stayed beautifully chilled outside the tent in the cold weather. I adore cereal in the morning with deliciously creamy milk.

Again, it was two hours before I was packed up and ready to go. The tent was still wet and therefore heavy and I could feel the extra weight on the bike.

Today was very much a day of three thirds. The first third was largely enjoyable despite the weather. I'd managed to pack everything up in dry conditions however the rain inevitably started the second I set off on the bike. Cycling downhill for the first few miles did not help me stay or get warm so I was grateful for the uphills when they arrived to generate some body heat. They were incredibly steep in places, sometimes up to 18% and 20% gradients. I was used to much easier ascents in the French Pyrenees and Alps. These Swiss hills and mountains were really hard work and reminiscent of the steep climbs in the Yorkshire Dales.

I bought provisions as I passed through the small village of Hemburg before descending again and then cycling across many fields in vast valleys surrounded by what I imagined to be mighty and rocky mountains. However, they were, of course, completely engulfed in fog. It seemed quite tragic that I was on the Alpine *Panorama* route and therefore the views should have been spectacular. However the weather was denying me these stunning views on a daily basis.

The second third of the day was extremely tough going. I'd reached the village of Glarus by 2pm, which would have been the end of my ride on this route today. Unfortunately, the nearest campsites were 10 miles away at the top of a long and very steep climb and I was booked into one of them. If I'd known how challenging and long the climb was going to be, I would probably have been defeated before I started and simply looked for a hotel in Glarus. Blissfully unaware, however, up, up, up I went.

Despite the climb, because it was so wet and because I was making such slow progress, I did actually get very cold. It was no surprise to see snow on the ground when I eventually reached the top. We were 900 metres (2,953 feet) high. Maybe all the surrounding peaks were snow-capped. I have no idea, I couldn't see them through the thick fog. The fabulous surprise as I reached the top was the stunning Klontalersee, a beautiful lake fed by many impressive waterfalls. It was hauntingly beautiful and that incredible shade of turquoise peculiar to Alpine regions.

Checking the map Swiss Trails had put together for me, I continued to the campsite 4 miles further along the lake. At least pedalling on more or less flat terrain again started to warm me back up a bit.

At the campsite, however, there was no sign of my panniers and the camp owners were not expecting me. Neither did they have any space to put me, they were full. I was cold, wet, tired and increasingly hungry. The light was also starting to fade. I called the emergency Swiss Trails number but, due to the poor mobile signal, was cut off from them before we'd been able to ascertain what had gone wrong. Fortunately, the campsite owners were tremendously helpful. They used their computer to translate everything they were trying to tell me on Google Translate and also called Swiss Trails themselves on the landline. Although Swiss Trails had put the name and address of this campsite on the details they had provided me with, they had actually booked me in at the campsite on the other side of the lake.

Thanking these campsite owners very much for their assistance, I wearily set off again on the bike and pedalled the 4 miles back to where I started and then cycled another mile or so further on to my actual campsite for the night. Everything was absolutely soaked – me, my bike, my tent. I did my best to dry the inside of the tent with a fairly wet tea towel. There were no fabulous facilities here as there were at Bachli last night. I had to pay an additional CHF1.50 for a shower and, if I wanted hot water to wash my hands or the dishes, it was another CHF1.50 each time. It felt so cheeky. The facilities were not even that pleasant. To reach the shower block, you had to walk through the large beer tent which was thick with cigarette smoke.

I definitely needed a hot shower so reluctantly paid the extra. The shower was at least powerful with plenty of hot water and definitely helped restore me.

And so began the third- third of my day. There was no café or any food to buy at the campsite and no cafes or restaurants anywhere nearby. Fortunately, I was able to dip into some of the supplies I'd brought from the UK and heated up a fabulous and toe-warming vegetable biryani, adding some chopped fresh vegetables to this wonderfully spicy dish. I positively glowed after eating it, feeling thoroughly nourished and warmed through.

Trangia camp stoves are storm-proof, which was proving essential in the weather I was encountering. Just as I finished eating, the heavy rain became a substantial deluge. I happily left my pots and pans outside to get washed and cleaned as much as possible by the rain whilst I stayed snugly warm inside my tent drinking a steaming hot mug of tea.

I didn't like leaving my precious bike outside in such heavy rain. At Bachli, I'd at least been able to store it under the shelter. I couldn't do anything about it though. I read my Kindle for a short while before giving in to another early night. To stay warm, I nestled down in both my sleeping bag and sleeping bag liner and was wearing my pyjamas, fleece bodywarmer, a Beanie hat and my fluffy bed socks (yes, I know, another luxury, but now essential, item). I'd cycled 48 miles at just under 10mph average.

Chapter 9 – Sunday 22nd July 2012: Cycling from Klontal to Fluelen

It can be quite tough dragging yourself from a luxuriously warm sleeping bag out into a freezing cold morning, but it had to be done. The sooner I set off pedalling, the sooner I would warm up again.

Despite some prolonged deluges during the night, it was dry when I awoke this morning. The tent was still unfortunately soaking wet when I packed it away. I tried to dry off my bike as best I could and I checked the chain, adding some oil to ensure it ran smoothly.

I managed a comparatively quick get away with my get-up-to-pack-up time, including brekkie, now greatly improved to 1 hour 30 minutes. Progress!

With teeth chattering, I tried not to freewheel downhill too quickly for mile after mile, back to Glarus and Route 4. In the UK, I give anything for a long downhill to whoosh down and enjoy. I was simply trying to avoid hypothermia at this point. I knew I'd got a big climb ahead today, the KlausenPass at 1952 metres (6,404 feet). That would warm me up. It was also a longer day at 50 miles.

I stopped for tea and a banana at a hotel in Linthal before commencing the climb to the KlausenPass. The climb started with a few switchbacks on cobbled roads, which rattled the panniers and me a bit, and then there was a long ascent through a tunnel. I switched on all my flashing helmet and bike lights to ensure I was as visible as possible to cars that wouldn't be expecting me there. I had my luminous yellow jacket on as well. The tunnel exacerbated the sound of approaching cars, making the experience quite nerve-wracking. The roar of any traffic was deafening.

It was a relief when I re-emerged into fresh air and daylight. I really started to enjoy the climb and got into a steady rhythm on more gentle gradients than I had become accustomed to in Switzerland so far. I was surprised at how much traffic there was on the mountain and how few cyclists. I probably saw less than a handful of cyclists the whole way up. On my previous Pyrenees and Alps trips, the roads were filled with col bagging cyclists. Here, the roads were filled with never ending, death-defying motor bikers roaring their way up to the pass. They really jangled my nerves, zipping their way past me much closer than I would have liked, leaving me choking on their exhaust fumes. Normally, ascending a mountain col is quite a peaceful affair.

I'd never climbed a pass carrying a heavy load on the bike and I actually wasn't sure if I could do it. Part of the initial purpose of this trip was to see if I could do it. If I did manage it, that would open the door to many more opportunities for future tours. It was painfully slow chugging along and I was surprised that it gave me such a voracious appetite. I was stopping to eat roughly every half an hour. Fortunately, I was carrying plenty of bread, cheese, fruit, pastries and biscuits to keep me going. Water was also in plentiful supply from many fountains en route.

Onwards and upwards, slowly but surely, I wound my way further and further up the mountain. Was I starting to hallucinate or was the sun actually starting to come out? Crikey moses! I was actually starting to have some visibility on my ride and see the surrounding scenery. Wow, it was so beautiful! I could have done without seeing how far and high the road was snaking in front of me though, eek!

It felt a significant achievement to reach the top. The first 30 miles of my day had already taken a staggering 6 hours. I still had another 20 miles to go, although, of course, much of it was going to be downhill. Who cares, I'd just climbed my first col with a heavily laden touring bike!

To celebrate this achievement, my jelly legs and I stumbled into the mountain café where I was delighted to see apple strudel and custard on the menu. Sadly, it turned out to be a rather soggy, microwaved affair but, hey, I'd earned it so I enjoyed every mouthful and washed it down with lashings of tea.

Now for the descent! I donned all my Winter gear which meant I was wearing a long sleeved thermal, a t-shirt on top followed by my long sleeved windproof cycling cardi, my waterproof jacket, Rainlegs over my shorts, waterproof overshoes, a buff for my neck, a cap to keep the rain out of my eyes, fluffy fleece earwarmers and thick Winter gloves. I appreciated every single item. Although I'd cycled up in a mixture of sun and cloud, I was engulfed in freezing fog and icy rain as I descended. I had all my flashing bike and helmet lights on in such poor visibility. My teeth were chattering, I was shaking with cold. I'm not sure how I would have managed without all that extra kit. As noted earlier, I've suffered the onset of hypothermia in the past and am fully aware of the dangers of cycling in the mountains. Wearing good kit significantly helps mitigate these risks.

As I swooped and swooshed my way down the mountain, the weather started to improve and I hit pockets of warmth as I got lower and lower down. I have read that for every 100 metres climbed, the temperature drops by 1 degree. I was therefore gaining many degrees of temperature as I descended. The impact was noticeable and certainly welcome. As I reached the bottom, it was time to de-layer again and re-pack all my Winter kit. In the warm sunshine, I was comfortable enough in just shorts, t-shirt and my ever-faithful windproof gilet. It was then a very pleasant ride into Fluelen, my stopping point of the day.

Fluelen is a stunningly beautiful small town on the edge of a lake, the Urner See, and surrounded by towering rocky mountains. The sun was now fully out and I could finally see everything. Switzerland did look as impressive as I had imagined! Moreover, I was keen to reach the campsite to get the tent up and dried out as soon as possible in this lovely sunshine.

Those working at the campsite reception were not the friendliest people, in fact they were quite rude and dismissive. They claimed they were not expecting me and yet my panniers were sat in front of them waiting for me and I could see my name on their list. After some pointless faffing, they begrudgingly took me to my camping spot, the only one left on the site, and I pitched my tent in double quick time. The campsite was on a steep stepped slope down to the lake. Most campers seemed to be watersports enthusiasts, generally running around in wetsuits. It was undoubtedly an incredibly gorgeous spot and I whiled away much time simply looking out of my tent door at the fabulous view and letting the warmth of the sun wash over me.

At this campsite again, it was an extra CHF1.50 to have hot water for your shower. Switzerland isn't well known for being very hot so I'm not sure who would want to have a cold shower at a campsite. It seems a bit of a con to me. There were no individual basins for washing your hands or brushing your teeth here either, just a long trough so it was normal to see other people's spit flowing past when brushing your teeth. Nice.

I really fancied a huge plate of macaroni cheese for dinner but soggy noodles with my remaining fresh vegetables chopped in had to suffice.

It would have been nice to take a stroll later in the evening however, after wandering down to the lake and back, collapsing in a heap became my key priority. I had climbed my first mountain col on a heavily laden touring bike today and had earned a restful night. I read cycle touring stories on my Kindle until it got dark before enjoying another night of blissful deep sleep.

Chapter 10 – Monday 23rd July 2012: Cycling from Fluelen to Sarnen

Despite wearing lots of layers, I was absolutely frozen as I set off cycling this morning. My muscles were now sore and stiff after cycling for a number of days in the cold and wet and I generally ached everywhere. My hayfever had also kicked in so I awoke with eyes so swollen, I looked like I'd been punched. Furthermore, my hair was indescribable. I had no idea what my hair looked like without being blown dry and straightened every day. It was both enlightening and horrifying!

It was a struggle to generate any heat and warm up on this first section today. The narrow road seemed to be clinging on below the cliffs for dear life whilst running above the shore of the Urner See. This was apparently an old military road. Incredibly, the Swiss had still managed to provide a cycle path that was fully segregated from the road. Although the road was busy and noisy with plenty of traffic fumes to choke on, it did feel much safer on this segregated path. When travelling through tunnels, the cycle path even had its own hewn out sections completely separate from the traffic. It would have been unrealistic to expect a cycle route traversing an entire country to be able to avoid all main roads.

I felt delightfully happy to be cycling through Switzerland, carrying my home, experiencing this amazing country in the Summer months and gaping in awe at the extraordinary scenery. I knew I'd eventually warm up and that I'd soon be cycling once again on quieter roads.

I stopped in the small and pretty town of Brunnen for a morning cup of tea and a croissant. Whilst taking photos of the stunning lake and surrounding mountains, I was asked to leave the area by a policewoman. Crikey, surely I didn't look that bad! Apparently, this was a private area for passengers catching boats across the lake, although I found absolutely no evidence of this, there were no signs. Others seemed to be able to wander freely in this area. How baffling. I felt a blot on their perfect landscape. I was half embarrassed, half amused. Maybe my swollen eyes and mad hair were scaring people!

I had a lovely encounter whilst munching my picnic lunch, overlooking another lake further along the route. An elderly gentleman arrived on his shiny red moped to eat his lunch. He sat nearby, asking me questions in German about what I was doing. He had some broken English, which helped. He explained he had cycle-camped 4,000km from Sweden to Switzerland when he retired and my trip reminded him of his incredible experiences. He took a photo of me, the "English lady", and I took one of him standing proudly by his moped, which was clearly his pride and joy.

The sun was thankfully gaining strength as the day progressed. I was pedalling mostly on the flat now, which was helping to loosen off my tired muscles. I was grateful I had a shorter day of 31 miles. Part of my route was also by ferry across the Vierwaldstatter See from Gersau to Beckenried. It felt such an easy life compared to the last few days!

I was thrilled to arrive at my campsite in Sarnen so much earlier than usual at 2pm. This place was such a sight for sore eyes. I loved everything about it. It was a huge complex, which I don't usually like, but the atmosphere was fantastic and so friendly. The site was filled with active families of all generations taking part in every land and water-based sport you can possibly think of. It was a true pleasure to see all these generations doing so much together and thoroughly enjoying themselves.

The site was extremely well organised. I had a superb and spacious flat grassy pitch very close to the lake. I pitched my tent in full sunshine enabling everything to fully dry out naturally. I was also able to get a good clothes wash done and, again, everything dried before nightfall.

I was ready for a proper meal tonight and the extremely large campsite restaurant did not disappoint. I drooled as I watched the chef cook up a vegetable "Asian wok" stir fry in front of my eyes. He asked if I was hungry to which I obviously replied yes. I probably looked like I needed feeding up. He promptly added plenty more vegetables and noodles. What a fabulous meal! I wish I could cook like him, the flavours were sensational. And I certainly appreciated the volume of food.

I'd seen some puddings on display when I went into the restaurant earlier. Although I was genuinely full, I couldn't resist going back inside, just to take another sneak peak. My eyes were clearly bigger than my stomach and I agonised over the incredibly tempting mango cheesecake and the mouth-watering exotic fruit salad. What was I thinking, get both! Both it was. What heaven!

An evening walk was much needed after dinner to help all that food digest. I felt like I walked for miles and still hadn't left the campsite grounds. It was a beautiful evening and, now that Switzerland had emerged from the dense fog and rain, the country was everything I had imagined it to be. It was also reassuring to meet some really friendly Swiss people. The Swiss do tend to keep themselves to themselves but they are generally very nice when they do engage with you.

The sun, the scenery, my fabulous campsite pitch, getting everything dry, being warm, eating so well and meeting lovely people all helped me feel extremely relaxed and happy. Even my muscles were feeling less sore. It was almost like being on a real holiday!

Chapter 11 – Tuesday 24th July 2012: Cycling from Sarnen to Gwatt, Thun

Today would be my biggest yet at 66 miles with 2 mountain passes to climb. Unusually, there was a choice of either a shorter or longer route at about the halfway point, soon after the village of Sorenberg. I would need to keep an eye out for that and decide at the time came which route I would take. It would depend on the time of day and my tiredness levels. I knew I was hoping to take the longer route. I suspected this route may be more scenic and I felt I would be cheating if I didn't take it.

I opted for a reasonably early start this morning to ensure I could fit the miles and the climbs comfortably into daylight hours. It was generally taking me around 1 hour 30 minutes from getting up to getting off, however I reminded myself it wasn't a race and it was always nice to spend time relaxing over my favourite meal of the day, breakfast, with the incredibly creamy Swiss milk I had fallen in love with. This morning, breakfast felt particularly special overlooking the peaceful and picturesque Sarnen See whilst everyone else at the campsite continued to slumber. I quietly and efficiently packed up my panniers, loaded the bike and set off.

I cycled back into Sarnen, the town itself, and found my way back onto Route 4. Today's cycling was what the tour was all about for me. Demanding but do-able, a challenging distance (bearing in mind the ascents and the weight I was carrying), extraordinary scenery, fabulous weather and friendly people. And I just love, love, love being in the mountains. Two mountain climbs in one day, what a treat!

The first was the Glaubenbielenpass at 1,611 metres (5,285 feet). I got into a good rhythm on this climb and, knowing how far I had to go and what progress I needed to make, this gave me plenty of motivation to keep my legs turning. As I climbed onwards and upwards, the views overlooking the lakes towards Luzern were truly spectacular.

I won't deny I wasn't tired as I reached the summit. It had started to feel that I was never going to make it to the top. I had made it in good time though and was very happy with myself for continuing to pedal at a good pace. My lower back had been giving me a bit of grief on the way up. Some evil biting flies were also making a real nuisance of themselves. The blood pumping through my veins must have been a tasty meal for them.

A family were already at the top of the mountain, taking photos, having cycled up from the other direction. Upon seeing me with all my panniers, they burst into a spontaneous round of applause and ran over for a chat. I was bursting with pride and couldn't stop grinning widely at this wonderful show of cycling support and solidarity. The Mum spoke very good English and called me "tough". It is not a word used to describe me very often, so she became an instant friend! Her husband and two boys were equally impressed. Reviewing the rest of my route for the day, the Mum exclaimed in surprise at the 2nd mountain I planned to ascend. She strongly recommended opting for the shorter route after Sorenberg to save time and energy. I knew I needed to be sensible even though I was still very keen to attempt the longer route.

When it was time to make the decision about whether to take the shorter or the longer route, I still had plenty of energy and was feeling strong. I had made good time on the journey so far and was fully confident I could cope with the longer route. Although this route was mostly on the main road, it was not at all busy and the cycling was very pleasant in a lovely basin surrounded by towering mountains. The road went down one side of the valley and then came back up the other side in a large V shape. The shorter route simply cut across the valley to avoid this detour. On the way down, I benefited from a fabulous tailwind in addition to the slight downhill gradient. Inevitably, this meant a persistent headwind on the gentle incline back up the valley. I broke this part of the journey up by stopping to enjoy my picnic lunch in the shade of a copse of trees.

Schalleberg was my next climb reaching 1,167 metres (3,829 feet). This was a hard and often steep climb in the baking heat of the afternoon sun. What a change in weather from the early days of the tour. Despite my hot face, practically purple with the effort of climbing, I was enjoying the sun and the heat far more than the cold and wet. I refused to complain about the warmth! The evenings remained refreshingly cool, which was conducive to a good night's sleep, and early mornings were still surprisingly chilly.

Upon reaching the top of this pass, I knew I'd broken the back of today. This was a relief and felt a great achievement. The rest of today's cycling continued under powder blue skies and warm sunshine, through rolling green hills, past wooden chalets and what I can only describe as "Anchor butter cows". The scenery was still everything I had imagined and hoped Switzerland would be.

I was a little apprehensive at having to cycle through the busy city of Thun later in the day. However, with the super-efficient Swiss signposting and segregated cycle paths, it was considerably easier than I could have imagined. The Swiss have got their cycle network down to a fine art, the UK could definitely learn a huge amount from them.

With a little help from passers by, I found my campsite in Gwatt alongside the Thuner See. I enjoyed a first class welcome here. The chap on Reception was expecting me and had apparently "heard all about me". Fame at last! Unusually, my rear panniers hadn't yet arrived from Swiss Trails although I could, of course, still pitch my tent and brew up a cuppa. My clothes and toiletries were stored in my rear panniers so the only thing I couldn't do was have a shower until they arrived. When they did arrive a short while later, this same lovely chap actually closed Reception to deliver the panniers to me personally. How about that for friendly and amazing service?

The showers were hot and fabulous, worth the wait. Even better, they were at no extra cost! The campsite had a fridge, which really made my day. I would be able to buy lots of fresh vegetables on my rest day tomorrow that I could store here and what a comfort to know my milk would remain truly chilled overnight. I really started to appreciate the importance and luxury of fridges in our everyday lives. In these temperatures, it was not possible to keep anything cool for long.

I heated up a very delicious mushroom risotto on my trusty Trangia for my evening meal. This was accompanied with a fresh green salad. My camp cooking and meals were starting to get rather posh! It was a lovely treat at the end of an excellent day. After dinner, I strolled alongside the Thuner See and around the adjacent park to loosen my legs and enjoy the sheer beauty of the deep blue waters and surrounding mountains. As the night drew in and the annoying biting flies descended once more, I retreated to the sanctuary of my tent and another blissful night's sleep.

Chapter 12 – Wednesday 25th July: A Rest Day in Gwatt near Thun

How exciting – I'd built a rest day into my trip! A rare luxury compared to previous tours. Having extended this tour to 6 weeks, I had sensibly planned one day off the bike per week. My bum would certainly appreciate this if nothing else!

My hopes of a leisurely lay in were dashed as my stomach woke me up at my usual time of 7am demanding breakfast. A lovely big bowl of Weetabix, sultanas and deliciously creamy Swiss milk, freshly chilled from the campsite fridge, followed.

I set about doing normal rest day activities – getting the laundry done, checking over the bike, shopping for food, relaxing over a cuppa and pastry at the campsite café and strolling around the lake whilst admiring the scenery. Snow-capped peaks, including the Niederhorn and Jungfrau, were striking against the deep blue sky, high above the crystal clear waters of the Thuner See. It was a hot, sunny day and I felt incredibly happy.

I wanted to head into Thun in the afternoon to have a nosy around and I needed to buy a few bits and pieces. Keen to give my body and particularly my bum a rest from cycling and the saddle, I braved taking the local bus. Fortunately, everything you need to know is on the timetable board in every bus stop. I therefore knew exactly what ticket to ask for and could get the right amount of change at the ready. Everything the Swiss do seems so effortless and efficient. The bus even turned up at precisely the right time. It does help that their roads are nowhere near a choked as ours.

In Thun, I located their famous "double decker" street of shops. Quite fascinating. I was on a mission to find an adaptor for my English plugs, especially to recharge my Blackberry, which was my lifeline to the outside world and provided the ability to write a daily blog to let everyone know how I was getting on. The adaptor I had brought with me wouldn't fit into the plug sockets at all the campsites I'd been to. This was unexpected given I'd used it previously in Swiss hotels on cross-country skiing trips.

I succeeded in obtaining one and was then even more delighted to spot the Kummerley and Fry Swiss activity tourist map I'd been looking out for all tour so far. It clearly shows every one of the Swiss national cycle routes. This would not only help me know on the Alpine Panorama route but also in a couple of weeks' time when I would make my way up Route 7, the Jura route, towards northern Switzerland and the border with France.

Designated cycle routes rarely take you through populated areas for obvious reasons, which does mean it can be difficult to obtain items such as maps and plug adaptors. I also bought some paper to write to my Dad whilst sitting in a café alongside the swirling turquoise waters of the river. He hadn't yet joined the technology revolution and therefore couldn't access my blog to find out how I was getting on.

Thun was a very pretty city and easy to wander around. The enchanting fairy-tale castle stood high and proud above the town. The river was providing the main source of activity today with school children jumping off bridges and plunging into what I can only imagine were icy waters. Lots of us were stopping to watch them, attracted by their squeals of delight and sheer numbers. This was so different from the school swimming lessons of my day.

I utilised one of my true luxury items once back at the campsite – my Thermarest chair. It is an exceptionally lightweight piece of kit that enables me to convert my sleeping mat into a comfortable chair. Genius! I got myself comfy on the chair in my tent porch, chopped all my fresh vegetables for tonight's stir fry, one of my favourite meals, cooked and ate, all without having to move.

What a fabulous day. Although I had generally been on the go all day, it had been at a very relaxed pace and I had been able to get so much done that would normally prove difficult on cycling days. I also felt suitably restored to take on the next stage of the trip.

Chapter 13 – Thursday 26th July 2012: Cycling from Gwatt to Fribourg

What a difference a rest day makes! The day dawned hotter, sunnier and clearer than ever. The mountains protecting the lake looked extraordinary in the early morning light, their snow-capped peaks the purest, sparkling white against the deepest blue sky. I couldn't help but smile. I felt refreshed, rejuvenated, re-energised and ready for the day ahead.

Off I pedalled in my happy, daydreaming state, enjoying the warm sun and the incredible scenery. It was easy cycling back through Thun, picking up and following the Route 4 signs. As I continued to cycle along, it dawned on me that I was actually retracing my route from yesterday. That couldn't be right? Oh bother! All the Swiss national cycle routes can be completed in either direction. I was following the Route 4 signs the wrong way and back to where I'd started! Pay attention, Lonnen!

I therefore had to cycle all the way back through Thun again, which was by now considerably busier and more tricky to navigate through all the traffic. Never mind, I was at least back on the right route now.

I had such a fantastic day on the bike. I seemed to have found my mountain legs, much needed as there were some really meaty climbs today, sometimes with up to 4 chevrons on my map! In the absence of a key, I assumed these to be a whopping gradient of over 20%. I still managed to cycle up all of them. I find it so much harder to walk and push a bike uphill, particularly carrying panniers, so I generally cycle up them albeit not at a great speed. People have been known to saunter past as I've battled uphill at less than 3mph!

It helped that I also found a village grocery store and bakery en route where I was able to buy plenty of juicy fruit, much needed in the increasing temperatures, in addition to their lovely bread. I was able to buy some local Gruyere cheese for lunch. I would be passing through Gruyere, the village famous for making this cheese, tomorrow. The fresh, cool water from the plentiful water fountains were also a godsend in the heat.

The temperatures had soared into the 30s during the afternoon. I was in a state of pure happiness, I love the sun and warmth.

I know these temperatures don't suit everyone. I'm just so used to very cold, wet cycle tours and this was a very big and much needed improvement. The lush greenery of the land contrasted fabulously with the deep blue of the sky. This really was sensational cycle touring.

Overall, I enjoyed an excellent 40 miles cycle today and had plenty left in the tank as I joyfully freewheeled my way down the most wonderful descent for miles into Fribourg, arriving by mid afternoon. I'd read that the river Saane running through Fribourg separated German and French speaking Switzerland. I was still astonished at how abrupt it was.

I was booked into the city's Best Western hotel tonight and was delighted to spot it literally as I entered the town. I tentatively offered a "guten tag" to the ladies on the reception desk, which was returned with a "bonjour". I speak much better French than German, although my French seemed to desert me at this precise moment. I bumbled along vaguely making myself understood, finishing with a hearty "danke". I needed to get my brain in gear – I'd already set off the wrong way this morning and now speaking a few sentences in a variety of languages! The staff on reception did not speak a jot of German or English. How on earth do they speak to their neighbours across the river?

Swiss Trails had already delivered my rear panniers and the hotel had thoughtfully and kindly taken them up to my room. Although I adore camping, it was so very lovely to have my own room for the night. It had everything I needed including, joy of joys, a kettle to make as many cups of tea as my heart desired! The room was superbly cool and there was plenty of space for all my luggage. An en-suite felt a considerable luxury. I was really looking forward to the opportunity to eat out again tonight. I didn't think it particularly appropriate to rustle up something on the camp-stove in my room.

After showering and changing, I went back out into the baking heat of the afternoon to explore Fribourg. It was a very pretty city and, according to my guidebook, one of the largest medieval towns in this region. I admired impressive 15th century Gothic facades as I strolled around as well as the 74-meter high tower and beautiful stained glass windows of the Cathedral of Fribourg. There were gorgeous narrow alleyways with tightly packed rows of little boutiques, antique shops and cafes. My favourite view was back along the bridge overlooking the deep gorge down to the river. It was simply breath-taking.

I indulged in a leisurely pot of tea, despite ordering once again in German instead of French. The afternoon heat was bouncing off the pavements and my feet welcomed the rest as I sat and watched the world go by. As a university town, Fribourg was lively and cosmopolitan and I'd chosen a great people-watching spot.

I had much more success with my language skills at the pizza restaurant in the evening, remembering to order everything in French. I felt utterly content at this wonderful restaurant which oozed charm and character. I'm a really early eater and was their only customer for quite some time. This resulted in very dedicated service. I indulged in the tastiest mushroom pizza and a fresh green salad with, naturally, a chilled glass of dry white wine. I was in heaven!

Chapter 14 – Friday 27th July 2012: Cycling from Fribourg to Enney (Gruyeres)

Another fabulous scorcher of a day! The mileage was disappointingly low again with no mountain climbs. I'd expected more mountain climbs on the "Alpine Panorama" route. Route 4 was still an exceptionally pretty one and very typically Swiss. Some of the climbs reminded me of the Yorkshire Dales in that they were very steep. I personally find this harder than the long drawn out ascents of the French Alps and Pyrenees that I'd previously encountered.

After a fabulous eat-as-much-as-you-want breakfast buffet at the hotel this morning (something I took full advantage of), I experienced great difficulty finding my way out of the city of Fribourg. The signposting seemed to vanish at the most critical points, e.g. roundabouts and junctions, leaving me with little or no idea where to go. Neither my maps nor books had any detailed maps or descriptions on how to get out of the city. It was quite frustrating, especially in the morning heat, choking on the fumes of the noisy, heavy traffic. When I finally made it out into the suburbs of Marly, I could start to breath and enjoy myself again. I knew I was back on the right track and the odd Route 4 signpost appeared, providing that much-needed reassurance.

I always felt much better once I'd found somewhere in the morning to buy my daily provisions and was therefore delighted to spot a Lidl as I cycled through Marly. Previously, I'd been coming across the baker/grocery store format typical to villages in this region. In these stores, I could always buy all the essentials for the day. The service was always friendly and first class. The food was consistently of a superb quality although inevitably expensive. This is Switzerland. I did love these stores and they were the hub of village life. In the more densely populated area that I was cycling through this morning, I had not come across any such stores. I knew Lidl could provide what I needed and at roughly one-third of the usual cost. What a bonus!

As well as a low mileage day of 31 miles, the route was fairly easy with short ups and downs even though some of the climbs were steep. Throughout Switzerland so far, I'd cycled through traditional, established hamlets and villages with history, character, spirit, heart and soul. Today, I was starting to pass through new villages that were not even on my map where apartments were being built in place of the usual chalets. Although smart in appearance, these new villages seemed so empty, devoid of people and life. The masses of flowers that normally tumble from every window, home and garden were not to be seen here. There were also no facilities to support these new homes – no church, no bakery, no school, no doctors, no shops, no nothing. This seemed so sad in such outstandingly beautiful scenery. The Swiss economy is performing better than most in Europe during this prolonged recession and there was certainly evidence of extensive construction activity from this region onwards. I know countries have to develop and expand, it just felt so out of place here.

Cycling through Gruyeres and the local region was a particular highlight today. Route 4 took me alongside the picture perfect Lac de la Gruyere before reaching Broc, where the original Nestle chocolate factory is located. It is a huge white industrial building in the middle of nowhere and the perfect spot for chocolate making with so many lush pastures and plump cows. Again, the green of this land made a startling contrast against the deep blue sky.

A few miles further along was the very well preserved tiny medieval city of Gruyeres perched on a hilltop and surrounded by completely unspoilt Swiss mountains. It is hard to take in the wonder and beauty of such places. It is like looking into an incredibly scenic painting and then realising that it is actually real! The only small blots on this picture-perfect landscape were increasing numbers of cars. The serene lake, the chocolate factory and Gruyeres all attracted tourists and money into the area. The Swiss did well to preserve everything so brilliantly. All the car drivers were very considerate when overtaking me so I can't complain.

A lovely campsite awaited me later in the day, nestled at the bottom of a long descent and hidden away from the main road. With no facilities for families such as swimming pools here, it was delightfully peaceful with mostly adults on site. I did have to pitch on slightly lopsided, lumpy ground and there were ants EVERYWHERE.

I needed to cycle a mile back up the hill to the small shop there, which was fortunately still open. As was often the case, there were almost no fresh vegetables. I was able to buy a tiny onion, a carrot and a good sized tomato. I also found a can of peas with a ring pull. Awesome! This would give me the opportunity to test the can opener on my new (and first ever) penknife. If it didn't work, I still had the ring-pull option as Plan B.

I cooked up all these vegetables with a packet of tasty mushroom couscous whilst being maliciously bitten by ants. Ant bites really do sting but there didn't seem to be any way of escaping them. I kept my tent firmly sealed even though some of the blighters still managed to get in. I am delighted to report that the can opener on my penknife was incredibly easy to use and I also used the "wood saw" (what??!!) to slice my fresh tomato. I was confident I wouldn't be using this to actually saw any wood!

Despite the ant bites, I once again felt completely content. I was cycling and camping in the most extraordinary scenery on this tour. After dinner, I went for a wander along the valley in the fading light, unable to stop craning my neck skywards to admire the extraordinary beauty of the majestic mountains in this perfect setting. In fact, it was a perfect evening.

Tomorrow would be my last day on Route 4. It seemed to have gone so quickly. I was so glad I'd had the opportunity to extend my tour, I would have felt very sad if I knew my cycling holiday was coming to an end so soon.

Chapter 15 – Saturday 28th July 2012: Cycling from Enney to Chessel via Aigle

I had an unusual night of disturbed sleep. I dreamt that millions of ants were crawling all over me and I kept leaping up to brush them off. Then heavy rain arrived accompanied by thunder and lightening. This was a real surprise as there hadn't been a cloud in the sky when I settled down for the night nor had it been muggy. Despite feeling groggy with the lack of sleep, I was quite relieved when daylight broke. Eating a sizeable breakfast always gets me back on my feet!

This was my final day on Swiss National Route 4. It was a longer and hillier route than my last few days at just under 50 miles and it didn't disappoint. I was back to cycling in cloud, drizzle and murk again especially as I was climbing over 1,500 metres (4,921 feet). Visibility thankfully wasn't too bad so I could at least appreciate the scenery I was cycling through. As the route progressed, it became increasingly remote and wild with a substantial deterioration in the road surfaces. I was very off the beaten track. There were places en route that had suffered from some rock fall. As I cycled through one of these, I must have disturbed a bird or something and some small rocks and stones tumbled down the hill. If any had hit me, they would have really hurt and could definitely have damaged the bike. I proceeded carefully. I didn't have any mobile phone reception here and there were clearly no passers-by so obtaining medical assistance or any form of help would have been a real challenge.

Luckily, I'd stocked up well on food at a lovely village shop earlier in the day so had plenty to see me through this remote region. I even had the unusual treat of a homemade quiche to accompany my usual menu. Normally in Europe, ham is liberally added to every quiche meaning I can't indulge as a vegetarian. Some Europeans also bizarrely seem to think ham is vegetarian when I ask… Fortunately, this quiche was cheese, cheese, cheese. I appreciate cheese was a staple part of my daily diet and one might assume I was getting fed up of it by now. However, this couldn't be further from the truth. Local, fresh cheeses changed as I cycled through different areas and there was always a delicious new flavour to try. Today, I had bought goats cheese for my bread rolls. I'd somehow even managed a discussion in French at the deli counter regarding their selection of cows, sheep and goats cheeses. I was quite proud of myself!

Most of the gradients today were sensible although there were also some ridiculously steep ascents. When I was tackling a seemingly vertical wall, I did think this had simply been added to the route to ensure there was more climbing on the Alpine Panorama and that it was a really unnecessary addition. I'm glad I stuck with it though, as it led to the remote and wild valleys that made the day so special. One hamlet I came across seemed to be supplied by the local mountain railway. I heard a number of trains rumbling along the single track from time to time. I saw no cars throughout this particular area. I'm not sure it would have been possible for them to drive on these severely pot-holed and broken roads. I'm sure they'd have got stuck. I was just about able to get my bike along in some places. This did not help my rather sore bum!

The route passed the huge Lac de l'Hongrin which was deserted, save for a few fisherman who had endured a long and difficult drive from the other direction to reach here. It must have been worth it for them. Again, it felt unusual that they didn't wave at me or bade me good luck as I cycled along. Cycling is generally very sociable in the UK and even more so in France where you are practically revered.

The route swept back up into the mountains and through a military training area. Needless to say this area was also completely deserted. I've never cycled across so many bridges in so few miles, there were seemingly hundreds. This must have been an incredibly challenging area in which to build these roads and bridges, not to mention expensive.

The cycling was enjoyable and relatively easy, if quite chilly, on this part. Once I'd reached the highest point of today, I gasped in delight as, through the cloud, I could see what lay below. It was Lac Leman (Lake Geneva). By jove, I had nearly done it! I had nearly cycled across the whole of Switzerland via the Swiss Alps. I could see this extraordinary lake and could even hear the very faint hum of traffic far in the valleys below. I wasn't expecting to feel like this, it really felt to be a special and monumental moment. I almost felt a bit teary. Come on, Lonnen, I still had a long way to go!

After taking a few photos (which actually just look like clouds but I can see the silhouette of the lake and the pictures mean something to me), I commenced the descent. The early stages were too steep with too many switchbacks to take at any speed. Carrying panniers is also not conducive to swooping down mountain roads with the bike at the angle that Tour de France cyclists take. No, my descent had to be somewhat more gentile and considered.

Down, down, down, the temperature rising as I descended. The temperature on my bike rims was also getting dangerously hot so I stopped for a short while to let them cool off. I continued down, freewheeling through the steep slopes of the vineyards as I descended into Aigle. It was hard to concentrate on looking where I was going and braking whilst trying to admire the fabulous views. My hands were also starting to hurt from braking for so many miles.

Wow, here I was, in Aigle, the official end of Route 4. I would be sad to say cheerio to the Route 4 signs, they had been a great friend throughout my traverse of the Alpine Panorama. I would very much have liked to look around, however I needed to press on to reach Chessel, my destination for the evening. I wish even more now that I had been able to spend at least some time in Aigle as I recently learnt that our Olympic gold medal winner, Victoria Pendleton, had carried out a number of years of cycle training here. No wonder she became so strong and fit with the prolonged steep climbs surrounding the area.

I felt suddenly alone without my Route 4 signs. Fortunately, the way to Chessel was very straightforward and I simply needed to now follow Route 1. I love Switzerland and its cycle signposts! Much of this section of Route 1 was alongside a river. This should have been easy however I was into a tough and persistent headwind and my progress was therefore slow. Having mentally finished the ride, I found it pretty hard to keep going. My legs felt heavy and stiff pushing through the wind. People whizzing along in the opposite direction without a care in the world being pushed by their tailwind didn't help much either.

My campsite was several miles away from Chessel village, which unhelpfully had no shopping or eating facilities. The campsite didn't seem to be expecting me, even though they'd happily accepted delivery of my rear panniers, and they did not want to give me a pitch. Tired, weary and a little fed up, I told them to phone Swiss Trails whilst I put my tent up. It was sometimes hard managing situations such as this in a foreign language, particularly at the end of the day when I just wanted to get my home set up and to start relaxing.

I found myself a flat, grassy pitch and was surrounded only by mobile homes and motor homes. No-one else seemed to be actually camping at this campsite. You all know by now how much I love campsites that charge extra for a shower with hot water (not), and this site unfortunately fell into this category. It was an extra CHF1. Once I had got all my toiletries and evening clothes set up in my shower cubicle and got undressed from my cycling clothes, I discovered the token machine in my shower didn't work. Annoyed, I got myself dressed in my sweaty, smelly cycling clothes again and transported everything to the only other shower cubicle with a token machine, which I hoped would work. Thankfully it did. The hot shower soothed my tired muscles and mind and calmed me down. Washing away all the sweat and grime from the day is very therapeutic. Plus I end up smelling much better!

There was a tiny shop on the campsite. There was no fresh food again however they did have a can of green beans, which I now knew I could open with my whizzy penknife. I enjoyed these green beans with some pasta accompanied by some tomato sauce. The shop also sold biscuits. Phew! I'd just about run out of biccies and didn't want to be without. That would indeed be tragic and significant levels of irritability would undoubtedly follow!

I thoroughly enjoyed my dinner. It was warmer back down in the valley with some sunshine and clouds. I went for my now usual evening walk around the area, again marvelling at the breathtaking beauty of the mountains. My legs felt a lot happier and less stiff and heavy afterwards.

I've now cycled across Switzerland making this the 3rd country I'd cycled across. I'd cycled across the UK doing Land's End to John O'Groats in 2007 and then traversed the length of France from Calais to the Mediterranean in 2009. I'd also cycled from the Mediterranean coast of France on the East to the Atlantic coast on the west via 28 cols on the Raid Pyrenean in 2010. I needed to find another country to cycle across, this was great fun!

I knew I'd got a long cycle to my friend, Mary's, tomorrow. Her, her husband Rene and baby son Max live in Saint Cergues close to Geneva. I'd arranged to meet Rene in Yvoire on the shores of Lac Leman and he would cycle back with me. So I couldn't relax just yet however I knew I then had another rest day coming up. Fabulous!

Chapter 16 – Sunday 29th July 2012: Cycling from Chessel, Switzerland to Saint Cergues, France

Wow, what a thunderstorm last night! I'd heard the distant rumblings of thunder as I was drifting off to sleep. Violent thunderclaps, vivid flashes of lightening and heavy rain woke me up a short while later. I find it quite exciting camping in storms, although it can be a bit unnerving with just a flimsy piece of nylon separating you from the elements. I was tired after so little sleep the previous night, so I put my eyeshades on, ducked down further into my sleeping bag and somehow managed a fairly decent night's sleep.

I foolishly thought it would be completely flat cycling along the shores of Lac Leman. How wrong could I be. Not only did the roads continually roll up and down, I was still contending with that fierce headwind. I was also now carrying my rear panniers in addition to the front panniers, rack bag and handlebar bag. It did make some difference to the weight although I actually felt much better balanced as a result. I generally find the bike rolls better with weight, although I could have been making this up to make myself feel better. Despite the cycling being hard work, I remained focused on the prize of seeing my friends later in the day.

I certainly passed through some exceptionally pretty villages along the shores of the lake and some extraordinary mansions. This helped keep me distracted. I would be passing from Switzerland into France today, although I wasn't sure at which point exactly this would occur. Surprisingly, given the extensive cycle network signs throughout their country, Switzerland can be terrible at telling you where you are. At the opposite end of the spectrum, you are rarely left in any doubt in France as to exactly which village you are in. I hoped that would be the case I cycled in and out of the two countries along the lake. I had been my usual organised self, having two different purses containing the two different currencies at the ready.

I stopped in a lakeside village with a bakery to buy my usual bread and pastry provisions. I was ecstatic to see several varieties of homemade quiche again, hurrah! It took quite a while to get the attention of the lady running the bakery and tea-shop. Apparently, wandering straight past me with a cursory nod and then proceeding to do the washing up was far more important than serving a paying customer. When she finally headed over to serve me with a sigh, I asked about the varieties of quiche. Even though it was obvious my French wasn't brilliant, she proceeded to run through them all at great speed in rapid fire French. I translated what she said as quickly as I could. I thought she'd said that one was a pear quiche, which was slightly baffling, until I realised she'd said "poivre" for pepper and not "poire" for pear. I clocked onto "epinard", which is spinach, and asked if it was completely vegetarian. She nearly spat the word back at me saying of course it was vegetarian. I double-checked it had no ham. What a comical reaction this provoked! Her arms were waving, her eyes were rolling, she sounded exasperated. How awful it must be dealing with a complete imbecile such as myself, I thought in amusement. She was being extremely rude and it was tempting not to buy anything at this point. I continued regardless, deciding being rude was her problem and not mine, and thoroughly enjoyed my fully vegetarian, homemade spinach quiche a little later on. What a palava just to buy a quiche! It was a wonder she had any customers at all.

I collapsed further down the road on a welcome bench overlooking the choppy lake for a morning break. I had reached the town of Evian, famous for its pure waters that are sold around the world. I only experienced a small part of the town and found it to be both wonderful and disappointing. I was surprised that it was a town of such size. This inevitably brought a lot of traffic and tourists, which seemed to ruin it a little, however it was possible to appreciate the grandeur and wealth that Evian water had brought to the town. Some of the buildings were phenomenal. I couldn't hide from the volume, noise or fumes of the traffic, although in true French (and Swiss) style, there was good cycling provision on a wide cycle path , keeping me safe and segregated.

After eating a few biscuits to perk me up, I cycled onwards into the debilitating headwind as well as the increasingly heavy traffic. I realised it was another nearby lake, Lake Annecy, that had a lovely cycle path all the way around it which was completely separate from the road. That route would have been much easier than this! Never mind. I needed to press on to reach the exceptionally pretty, medieval village of Yvoire where I would be meeting Rene around lunchtime.

I arrived in Yvoire in good time and was able to collapse on another welcome bench to eat my hard earned spinach quiche. I didn't have long to wait before Rene arrived, with a big beam on his face. He couldn't believe how much weight I was carrying on the bike! He was on a lightweight racing bike without so much as a small bag.

I had pre-warned him this could be a slow ride home, not something he was used to. However, as we wound our way through the country lanes towards his home in St Cergues, he seemed to quite enjoy ambling along at my steady touring pace, chatting away. Although Rene took me the flattest route he could find, I became slower and slower the further we went. The tiredness had really taken hold now. I'm sorry, Rene! He was probably wondering how I'd made it across the Swiss Alps and how I planned to do several more weeks of cycling. I needed to get off the bike and rest, rest, rest. This was the most shattered I'd felt all trip.

I nearly cried with relief as, several miles later, we rounded the final corner and pedalled up to their house. And there she was. My good friend, Mary, stood in the driveway, smiling, and holding 8 month old Maxime in her arms. It was the first time I had met gorgeous Max. He appeared completely unruffled by the arrival of this rather sweaty, emotional and exhausted stranger on his doorstep. More importantly, he had lots of smiles for his Auntie Andi! Maybe I looked comical to him in my dishevelled state!

Right, first things first. Shower? No. Laundry? No. Get the tent out to dry? No. Carrot cake and catch up? YES! Mary bakes the most incredible carrot cake on the planet. We indulged in two hefty slices and a marathon chatting session. I apologised for sitting in my smelly cycling clothes as we caught up but Mary laughed that she was used to it when Rene arrived home every night from his cycle commute from Geneva.

The cake and catch up had given me the energy to think about showering, doing the laundry and getting the tent out to dry. I laughed when I walked into my bedroom with all my panniers. Having kept up to date with my blog and read about the shenanigans I'd had at Eurostar, getting my precious gas canisters confiscated, Mary had very thoughtfully bought me some gas canisters which were waiting for me on the bedside cabinet. What an absolute star! We'd discussed how difficult they were to obtain in France before I'd set off and she'd located some at her local Decathlon store. Thank you Mary!

Showering felt like absolute heaven and wrapping up in a soft fluffy towel afterwards was pure luxury. I'd got used to my quick dry camping towel, which certainly did the job and was very practical, but there was definitely no element of indulgence with it.

Mary and I took Max for an afternoon stroll in the pushchair for a quick sleep. (I had been tempted to trade places with Max so that I could sleep in the pushchair instead.) The walking helped loosen off my tired legs. Mary's life had changed so much since we'd last seen each other and we continued to natter and swap stories as we walked.

It was so good to be back with Mary and her family. I couldn't have received a warmer welcome. Their home is amazing, sat peacefully in the hills above the village of St Cergues, their sun-soaked terrace and pool overlooking both Geneva and the Jura Mountains in the distance. I sat lazily watching the aeroplanes going to and from Geneva airport many miles away whilst dinner was being prepared.

And what a fabulous dinner it was! Roasted peppers stuffed with lentils, tomatoes and mozzarella accompanied by a big salad with a fabulous dressing made by Rene. This was followed by 3 – yes, 3! - desserts! This was undoubtedly better than any of my camp cooking efforts!

I was thoroughly relaxed and happy. As I snuggled down in my real bed for the night, I looked forward to a deep sleep and a much needed rest day tomorrow.

Chapter 17 – Monday 30th July 2012: Rest Day in Saint Cergues

I can't tell you what an utterly relaxing and truly superb day I had at Mary's. So much so, in fact, that I decided to stay for another day. I was surprised at how tired I was and, given I had several more weeks of cycling, it made sense to give my body a good rest. I couldn't pass the opportunity to spend more time with Mary and Max either. I'd barely seen my good friend since she'd moved abroad and Max was so incredibly adorable, I was loving playing temporary Auntie for a short while!

I had the most perfect breakfast outside on the terrace by the pool, lazily enjoying the warm sunshine on my skin. And then, PLOP! A half dead fly landed on my head and rebounded into my cereal. Well, that kind of ruined the moment! I had to laugh.

Mary and I had a lovely morning, playing with a delighted Max and eating yet more carrot cake. I then helped her make a spinach and ricotta quiche for lunch which we ate with salad left over from last night. Food was featuring rather heavily during our time together. Clearly nothing had changed much since Mary had left the UK!

We explored the wonder that is Decathlon in the afternoon. I gazed at the shelves of screw-top gas canisters, willing myself to squeeze yet more into the panniers but alas, I simply didn't have the space or ability to carry any more. I did, however, buy a bargain priced 8 euro pac-a-mac with a hood. It was a wonderfully lightweight piece of kit that packed down very small. Although not fully breathable, I only needed a non-cycling waterproof jacket to run to and from the campsite shower block or nearby local shops in a deluge. The jacket I was currently carrying with me was an excellent one, just much heavier than this that I was now buying. Mary and family were returning to the UK later in the week and were happy to take my existing jacket back with them (thank you again, guys!) along with some other bits and pieces that I no longer needed, including my Swiss Route 4 guidebook and my pegless clothes line (there was never anything to attach it to).

We also popped into a nearby giant hypermarket, which made my eyes boggle. Having struggled to buy much in the way of fresh fruit and vegetables en route from local village shops, I was in paradise in their enormous fruit, vegetable and salad section. My mouth then watered in the bakery and pastries section. Oh, the tempting smells of freshly baked breads! There was aisle after aisle of yoghurts, cheeses and desserts. I felt like a big kid running around exploring this new piece of heaven. I bet it was easy to overspend considerably here all the time. I wanted to buy everything!

Once back home, dinner was another fabulous affair: savoury pancakes with mushrooms, spinach, onions, cheese and a big salad. Mary was inspiring me greatly to try much harder with my own cooking at home. I usually stick to the same small number of dishes, which I enjoy, but I needed to spread my wings and try some new things.

Despite being a shattered new Mum, Mary then spent the rest of the evening with me investigating campsites in the region of the French Alps I would next be touring through. Being an organised sort, I had always pre-booked campsites previously, never leaving it to chance. Just turning up at campsites would be a brave new step into unknown territory for me. At least being able to locate potential campsites on the internet softened the blow. In fact, they all looked so lovely, I was getting excited again at the next stage of my trip. We agreed to call the sites tomorrow to double check they would be able to fit me in during the busy Summer holiday season.

But first, I had another blissful day of rest to look forward to tomorrow. It would be hard to give up being looked after so incredibly well. I felt fully pampered and was certainly eating better than I had ever done in my life. Even my Blackberry and Kindle were now as fully recharged as I was!

Chapter 18 – Tuesday 31st July 2012: 2nd lazy rest day in Saint Cergues

Today was another fabulous rest day with Mary and Max. There were no suicidal flies nose-diving into my cereal this morning, thankfully. As Mary and I nattered away over an extended breakfast on the terrace, Max joined in with his baby chatter. It was so cute!

Mary very kindly called the campsites I planned to visit for the next part of my tour to ensure they would be able to fit me in over the next few days. Almost without exception, they responded that they would always find space for a cycle camper. Feeling marginally relieved, I hoped so.

Later in the morning, we had a trip out to the local garden centre. I was able to buy a miniature bottle of lavender oil. I take lavender oil with me whenever I travel and especially when camping. It makes the tent smell much nicer, I put it on my pillow to help me sleep, I massage it onto tired muscles and it especially helps relax my arthritic neck. I'd somehow managed to bring out a bottle of rose oil on this tour. I didn't even know I had a bottle of rose oil! Nice as it was, it was lavender oil I craved, so I was delighted to be able to finally buy some.

We went for a stroll around the village of Jussy afterwards. Mary was really starting to suffer with the heat. We planned to get some ice-creams or go to a café, but we had crossed over into Switzerland and neither of us were carrying any Swiss Francs. Agh! However, the promise of a refreshing swim in their pool when we returned helped keep us all going.

"Refreshing" was one description of their unheated pool. Mary and Max were already cooling down in the water, Max chuckling away and splashing around. I had made it in up to my ankles, shocked at how icy-cold it felt. It was a tremendously hot 33 degrees and yet my skin was starting to turn purple with cold as I attempted moving further into the pool. I was by now up to my knees and had already lost the feeling in my frozen feet. Mary and Max, in the meantime, were fully submerged with just heads happily bobbing above the water.

Anyone who knows me will tell you how I suffer with the cold. This seemed ridiculous, though. It was a hot, sunny day! I eventually made it into the pool up to my waist, my teeth chattering as we entertained Max, splashing a ball around. I retreated to the terrace after a short while and before body parts started to drop off. Mary later declared herself thoroughly restored after her "refreshing dip". I was just starting to get the blood back into my toes!

We ate vast quantities of more excellent food throughout the day. Dinner was another fantastic creation of couscous and masses of roasted vegetables with a gorgeous dressing. I adore plate loads of veggies and, given fresh food had been either hard to come across or hard to keep fresh in the heat whilst on tour, this was absolute nirvana for me.

I ran through my plan for the next few days during the evening. I had selected a tour from a cycling guidebook of the French Alps. I'd already cycled a small section of this region in the previous year with Bike Adventures and would even be tackling one of the same cols again. I wondered how different it would be to climb it on a fully laden touring bike this time. I guess I would soon find out.

Thanks to the wonderful hospitality of my fabulous friends, I was now fully relaxed, restored, recharged, refuelled and ready for off.

Chapter 19 – Wednesday 1st August 2012: Cycling from St Cergues to Abondance

It seemed appropriate to start the next stage of my tour on the 1st day of a new month. This was also a bank holiday in Switzerland therefore Rene had the day off work. He lived in France but worked in Switzerland. He was happy to escort me on his bike for the first few miles and up my first col for this part of the trip.

It was a lovely morning when we set off. I just about held myself together leaving Mary's. I'd had such an amazing time and I could feel myself welling up as I left. I promised myself I wouldn't get upset. Little Max wouldn't have been at all impressed if I had. So I was all smiles and waves as I said cheerio, despite the huge lump in my throat.

Cycling initially with Rene kept my mind focused as we chatted along the route. The first stage was on busy roads and we also stopped so I could buy provisions at a nearby bakery and mini-market. Fortunately, we then soon moved onto quiet roads and commenced the climb up Col du Feu (1,121 metres / 3,678 feet). I was back in France and it's fabulous gentle gradients. I got into a good rhythm carrying my heavy load, slowly chugging my way up the mountain. The mountain was covered in trees shading me from the growing heat of the sun. Rene seemed to be having a ball! He'd power up the hill and then freewheel back down to join me for a chat before zooming back off again. I was worried he wouldn't enjoy it, being usually such a speed demon, however he did seem to be genuinely happy. I certainly appreciated his enthusiastic company. It was also helpful cycling with someone who knew the way!

He needed to get back to help Mary pack for their trip back to the UK so we went our separate ways after descending the col into the pretty village of Lullin. He pedalled off with a big grin and at great speed whilst I sat down on a bench to devour a banana and a delicious pastry in the gorgeous sunshine. As with Switzerland, there were endless water fountains with plentiful fresh, cold water. Absolute heaven. I was also amazed to see a public loo, especially when I discovered it was a wonderfully clean English style toilet and not the squat style that still frequents areas of the French countryside.

After Lullin, my pace slowed as I took in the unbelievably stunning scenery I was cycling through. I felt the luckiest person alive to be experiencing all this. I don't have words to sufficiently describe the extraordinary beauty. I was in the Chablais region of the French Alps. It was so peaceful, the locals were so friendly and supportive, there were barely any cars on the road and the weather was fabulous. This was the life!

I was back down to earth with a bump as I came across my first completely closed road just 10 miles away from my destination. I cycled down the road anyway to see if it was passable on a bike, which very often closed roads are. This one was absolutely not passable and was fully barricaded to beyond the height of a lorry. I sat on a wall in the warm sunshine to eat lunch and contemplate my next step. Looking at the map, it seemed my deviation would be quite considerable. There are only so many roads that can be built in mountainous territory. I would need to cycle most of the way towards Thonon and Lac Leman and then head all the way back to end up a bit further down the road from where I was now sat.

The detour was 16 miles, the first few miles being on a main road with a downhill slant. The following few miles were all climbs. I was extremely grateful for the previous two rest days as my fresh legs were being tested now. This deviation doubled my anticipated climbing for the day and took an extra two hours of cycling. Can you imagine an extra two hours of squash, football or aerobics when you're tired? That's how I felt! A deviation of this length would barely bother a car driver however this was hard work for a fully laden touring cyclist towards the end of the day. I reasoned the weather was still fabulous and I knew I would rather be here than anywhere else. It was all part of my big cycling adventure.

All tour so far, I had been used to a plentiful supply of fresh, cold drinking water from village fountains. However, even though I was passing similar water fountains through these villages, they now generally had a firm "non-potable" (non-drinking water) label firmly stuck across them. How strange. These fountains had existed practically forever. Why was the drinking water suddenly not drinkable? This phenomenon is also happening across Spain where my Dad lives. He believes it's down to budget cuts during this worldwide recession. The water from these fountains would normally be regularly tested for safety by the local councils. This was clearly an easy area for the councils to cut costs by sticking a note on declaring "non-potable" and no longer having to carry out these safety checks.

I therefore had to start rationing the increasingly disgusting warm water in my plastic water bottles. The village of Chevenoz thankfully came to the rescue several miles later with crystal clear and perfect drinking water gushing from multiple fountains. I gulped bottle after bottle of cold water. It was thoroughly refreshing in the dry heat. Thank you Chevenoz!

The ride through the Gorges de la Dronse and the Abondance valley to the village of Abondance was very beautiful. My legs were aware the road had a continual and gradual uphill slant. The village of Abondance was exceptionally pretty with charming, traditional buildings oozing history and character and colourful flowers tumbling out of every home, shop, garage and bridge. It took me a couple of attempts to find the campsite, which I knew was here somewhere. It was a lovely small and friendly campsite with a number of other tents dotted around. I was getting used to most campsites not really having tents and being filled with motor-homes and caravans instead. I pitched under a shady tree and went to explore the village.

I was still overwhelmed that so many picture-perfect places exist and I seemed to be cycling through them all. These historic villages were a source of great pride to the French and were very well preserved. This place had a lovely atmosphere also. I stopped for a large chilled pink grapefruit juice at a café benefiting from the cool breeze created by the river surging alongside me. I relaxed and caught up on my diary writing. Today's cycle ride had been longer than expected, thanks to the deviation, at 48 miles and every pedal stroke had been worth it, as always.

I was able to buy some fresh vegetables for dinner from a local grocery store as I walked back to the campsite. Mary had wrapped me up the rest of the spinach and ricotta quiche we'd made and I couldn't wait to eat this with some boiled new potatoes and fresh carrots, courgette and green beans. I'd bought some fruit compotes at the supermarket with Mary yesterday so stirred this together with a chilled natural yoghurt for pudding before indulging further with lots of biscuits and my cuppa. Everyone who walked past looked suitably impressed at my feast and the ability of someone so slim to put so much away.

Thunder started to rumble in the distance as I was settling down for the night. I knew it was time to hunker down when the lightening started to flash and then the inevitable heavy deluge arrived. I happily nestled safely down in my tent, pulled my eyeshades on and, incredibly given the conditions, slept like a baby.

Chapter 20 – Thursday 2nd August 2012: Cycling from Abondance to Montriond

I knew today was a short one mileage wise, despite the small matter of one major climb up the Col de Bassachaux at 1,783 metres high (5,850 feet). I was therefore able to take my time getting up and ready for the day. A pleasant morning dawned with the sun burning off the thick mist left by the storm last night. Whilst eating breakfast, a very bright and cheerful chap approached and asked if I was English (what gave me away?). I was surprised, he was English himself and I'd not heard many English people for much of the trip. He was on holiday with his wife and young son and they were doing various outdoor activities. He loved the sound of what I was doing and re-lived some of his earlier days where he'd enjoyed camping and biking holidays in the Alps. It was a real boost having a chat with a fellow enthusiast.

Once I'd packed up the tent and loaded the bike, I pedalled a few yards around the corner….and then promptly stopped at the café for tea and a pastry. It's hard work this cycle touring life! I took the opportunity to stock up for the day from the lovely village shop, which seemed to sell everything in a small space. I wasn't allowed to buy any cheese other than their local Abondance cheese, such was their level of pride, and I was very happy to oblige. And, then, I finally did manage to summon the energy to set off properly.

It was a steady climb all the way to La Clusaz, normally a busy ski village, today a very busy Summer outdoor sports resort. There was a huge buzz about the place and I couldn't help but smile as I cycled through. It felt tragic to whoosh downhill for a couple of miles once I'd reached La Clusaz, thereby losing all that height I'd worked so hard to gain over the last few miles. However, this was the route I needed to take to then commence the climb up the Col de Bassachaux, one of the highest road passes in the Chablais. It was described in my guidebook as "a challenging climb up a very quiet road". The challenging climb was spot on however the road was not as quiet as I'd hoped. Maybe I was expecting too much.

This area is hugely popular with mountain bikers and boasts an extensive network of trails for every level. The mountain bikers were approaching their day in quite a different way to me.

They were taking the chairlifts up the mountain to then swoop all the way back down, albeit on technical trails. I, on the other hand, was battling on my fully laden touring bike up increasingly steep hills in hot sunshine. The average gradient of this climb is 9%, however the gradients early in the ascent are very gentle and they get steeper and steeper as you get higher and higher. The excitement of the mountain bikers all around me helped keep my own energy levels up and, again, no matter how hard it got, I knew I'd rather be here experiencing this than be anywhere else. This thought was tested as the final part of the climb did look and feel like a grey vertical wall, taking huge amounts of strength and effort, not to mention rather a few swearwords (sorry Mum!). I had become a hot and bothered, sweaty mess.

With so many people around came facilities, so there was cool, fresh water readily available, clean toilets and cafes. I didn't want to stop at a café until I'd at least completed the climb. Onwards and upwards to the very top where I suddenly heard an English voice bellowing "now THAT'S impressive!". It was the chatty English guy with his wife and baby son from the campsite this morning! Neither of us knew each other was heading up this col. What a wonderful surprise. We swapped stories of our mornings and wished each other well for the rest of our respective holidays.

I ate my picnic lunch with the delicious Abondance cheese in the best location ever. I was sitting on the top of the Col de Bassachaux overlooking the Lac de Montriond far in the valley below which was surrounded by the rocky peaks of the Aravis mountains in the distance. It was simply breathtaking. I wanted to share this with the world so posted this photo on the blog (details at the end of the book). I'm not a photographer, and I was using my Blackberry to take photos, but thankfully the photos took themselves. This view simply blew me away.

I had to tear myself away eventually and get a bit of a move on. To say the day's mileage was so short at 29 miles, I'd still got quite a long way to go. Admittedly, the next bit was downhill and should have been fairly quick. However, the guidebook explained that the paved road ended at the summit of the col and, to traverse the pass to Montriond, my destination for the evening, I'd need to cycle along a forest track for a few kilometres. Apparently even with slick tyres it was possible to cycle at least 75% of this off-road section.

I heartily disagree! I couldn't cycle on my touring bike with it's good tyres for at least 75% of it. It was shocking. It was all rocks and boulders, true mountain biking country. Even walking, bouncing and banging my bike down with all it's heavy panniers was incredibly challenging, very tiring and took a really long time. My poor arms and hands took a hammering trying to keep hold of the bike and it's enormous weight. It was hard to keep it upright, the weight of the panniers pulling the bike to one side or the other. Despite this, the views and the weather more than made up for any frustrations on the walk/bounce/bang descent. I also met some nice mountain bikers and hikers although they must have wondered what on earth I was doing in this terrain. If any further tracks were mentioned in this guidebook, I would certainly research alternative routes. These tracks were definitely not suitable for anything other than hardy mountain bikes.

Hurrah – I reached a paved road! I knew the village of Les Lindarets wasn't far away now with its wealth of cafes and shops. Fantastic, I needed a break after that descent. I stopped at one of the first cafes I saw and promptly ordered a milky tea with a chocolate crepe, one of my favourite treats in France (along with the sinfully gorgeous pain aux chocolats). The service was extremely friendly and I happily relaxed in the sunshine, chuckling about the rather crazy experience I'd just had.

A group of English people then arrived at the café, both adults and children. I felt so sad that they didn't attempt a single, solitary word of French – not even a cheery "bonjour" or a "merci". My French is not brilliant and my pronunciation is most likely terrible, but I will always have a go. The locals love you trying and will do their best to help you along themselves. The menu was all in French so they could have attempted some of the words rather than just ordering burger, chips and coke. They could have gone to Blackpool to do that!

Never mind, each to their own. It was time to continue. The part of Les Lindarets that I was currently in was at the bottom of the chairlifts. A short way further down the road was the actual village itself. Again, it was very busy with lots of people.

It was gorgeous! It was so unbelievably pretty and full of character. And, bizarrely, there were goats clambering freely everywhere: over cars, on the roofs of houses, drinking out of the water fountains, some were in the water fountains. It was crazy and fun with a wonderful atmosphere. My guidebook had warned me this place was nicknamed the "village of the goats". It was clear to see why!

My last few miles were spent whooshing downhill on blissfully smooth tarmac. My bike, panniers and bum really appreciated this. No rocks, stones or gravel in sight!

My campsite for the night was easy to find. Reception was not yet open although there was a notice, which I translated to mean pitch your tent wherever you like and sort out money later (I hoped). Fair enough!

Each pitch was a similar size and could fit a car, caravan and awning. My tiny 2-man backpacking tent looked absolutely dwarfed by the size of the pitch but it was great to have so much room all for me.

The two ladies on Reception squealed in delight when they saw me and understood what I was doing. They thought I was great. Crikey, my head would get big at this rate! I hadn't even done 30 miles today! They fired lots of questions at me, whilst munching their way through impressive chunks of cake, which I did my best to answer. They also directed me to the nearest supermarket a few miles away when I asked.

I pedalled down to the supermarket, unencumbered by panniers. What a difference in weight, although I could barely control the bike. I guess it is akin to the difference between driving a tank compared to a Smart car.

I still had a packet of mushroom risotto to heat up so bought some refreshing mixed lettuce leaves, which came with a sachet of balsamic vinegar, and some juicy cherry tomatoes to accompany it. I then saw some Tiramisu and added that to my basket as well. Nothing would last long in the heat and it was a huge treat to be able to enjoy salad as well as a chilled dessert. It felt like fine dining back at the tent. And all polished off with a large mug of green tea.

I was hopeful for a storm free night tonight. There was nothing remotely threatening in the sky before I went to bed but that didn't seem to mean anything here in the mountains.

Chapter 21 – Friday 3rd August 2012: Cycling from Montriond to Sixt Fer a Cheval

Thankfully, there were no storms or heavy rain last night. However, I was surprised to find myself waking up to a cool and cloudy day. I had slept so deeply, it was a real struggle to pull myself out of bed. In fact, it was a real battle just to escape my sleeping bag, I seemed to be very wrapped up and twisted around in it.

Thankfully, breakfast was as gorgeous as usual and was worth getting up for. I was onto nut-free fruity muesli now, adding a chopped banana and any other fresh fruit I had. The cooler night had kept the milk more chilled also, making everything much tastier.

Restored after re-fuelling, I knew it was back up the long hill into Montriond, where I could buy some provisions, before cycling into Morzine, the famous ski resort. I then had a very steep climb out of the village as I started the ascent up the Col de Joux Plane at 1,713 metres (5,620 feet). I could just about keep the bike upright as I pedalled below 3mph and slowly, slowly, ever so slowly inched my way up the mountain. It was both humorous and depressing to make no progress on the people hiking up the road in front of me.

But I got my first "chapeau" of the trip up this col, the highest cycling accolade from the French. What a boost! I love the French! They are so much friendlier than the Swiss. The Swiss are lovely on a person to person basis but there is no show of camaraderie or support on the road. In fact, I rarely saw other cyclists in the mountains in Switzerland at all. Here in France, every cyclist would shout some level of encouragement on the road. Quite often, people in cars would, too. In the past, I've had people driving past slowly with all the occupants giving me a round of applause and some even giving me food or drink. The French are wonderful.

The gradient eased as the climb progressed and I settled into a steady rhythm. Lots of cyclists came past. "How much weight?" one of them wanted to know. "Too much" I responded, having no idea how much weight I was dragging up the hill. "Bon courage" and "bravo" yelled many others as they powered past. I felt so happy and couldn't stop smiling, hugely encouraged by this wonderful support and cycling camaraderie. This is what I love best on the road. It makes me feel a part of an extended happy, friendly family.

As I approached the summit, a teenage boy struggled past with a face bright pink with effort. He had a huge smile and words of encouragement for me. His friend passed by a few minutes later. When I reached the top, both of them afforded me a round of applause. They dug into their pockets and gave me an energy bar (gosh, did I look that bad?!) for my efforts with lots of amazed head shaking and back slapping. I felt like a celebrity and was grinning like a loony! I thanked them hugely before commencing the descent before I got too chilled. My legs were shaking, partly with effort and partly with surprise and happiness at all the attention. I was absolutely loving the tour and living a dream.

I swooped and swooshed my way down the mountain switchbacks. About three-quarters of the way down, from the corner of my eye, I saw some picnic tables. An excellent spot for my picnic lunch, I decided. The tables were also bathed in the first and welcome sunlight of the day. I'd earned my fresh baguette, local cheese and juicy tomato and therefore thoroughly enjoyed my lunch.

The French and their obsession with food made me laugh. Many cyclists were huffing and puffing their way up the mountain and would always bade me good day. When they saw I was eating, they always, without fail, wished me "bon appetit". The world seems to stop for them where food is concerned. I don't blame them. Even the simplicity of their bread and cheese was an absolute feast. I really saw today that it was impossible for them to cycle past without wishing you bon appetit, no matter how out of breath they were cycling up an Alpine climb.

I completed the descent into the pretty town of Samoens and then had a very pleasant pedal along the Fer a Cheval valley and its spectacularly deep gorges. I was cycling to the campsite at Sixt Fer a Cheval, which was several miles further along and at the end of the road. It was a superb cycle in dramatic and awe-inspiring scenery. This route wasn't in my guidebook but the campsite had been recommended by one of Mary's friends and was definitely worth the detour. And then, wonder of wonders, I even overtook another cyclist as I approached the campsite!

I was amazed and delighted to see many other tents at this campsite. How unusual. As I've noted before, most campsites seemed to be filled with caravans and motorhomes. This site was in the most spectacular setting. We all had our necks permanently craned upwards to take in the magnificence of the deep gorge we were in. Photos could do this place no justice.

The pitches were lovely and grassy, which would make for a comfortable night. I stood back to check the tent was pitched properly and had to giggle. My bike was laid down in the grass next to my tent and looked exhausted! Another photo for the blog!

There had been no shops for miles so I was happy to see a little café near the entrance to the campsite. They were open into the evening. It was time to treat myself again. A huge fan of pizza and salad, I was able to indulge in my favourite dinner tonight with a glass of chilled white wine. Wine is so cheap in France, it costs little more than a chocolate bar. I was also able to buy some milk from them for breakfast tomorrow, even though they didn't officially sell it, which was quite a relief. They were incredibly accommodating and I wanted to give them a hug for making my evening so relaxing and wonderful!

Today's mileage had been short again at 25 miles although I couldn't have done much more with the climbs being so long and challenging. I prefer cycling and climbing in the mountains to simply mile munching. I was also in a nice routine by now and wanted to find and settle into a campsite by mid-afternoon every day. This then left me plenty of time to shower, wash and hopefully dry my clothes and towel, write my diary, cook, eat and wash up and then update the blog before going for a stroll, reading my Kindle and finally snuggling down for a good night's sleep. I sound a real creature of habit! I liked having a structure to the day and each day brought such different things that it never felt the same or routine anyway.

I wrote in my diary that I had a "lot of respect" for tomorrow's ride, which was code for being terrified! The route would be much longer than my last few days with the Col de la Colombiere as my big mountain climb of the day. I had cycled up the Col de la Colombiere on my Alps tour with Bike Adventures last year, although I had no recollection of which of the many cols we cycled that it was. The Tour de France had tackled it a few short weeks ago. My legs were tired from the short days so I wasn't sure how I would cope with tomorrow.

I felt confident. I knew I could do it if I put my mind to it. I knew it would help psychologically to set off early so I set my alarm and got ready for my big day ahead.

Chapter 22 – Saturday 4th August 2012: Cycling from Sixt Fer a Cheval to St Jean de Sixt

My getting-up-to-getting-off ritual in the mornings was by now reaching Formula One standards compared to my earlier endeavours. I was happy I could now achieve everything in half the time of before at around an hour in a chilled out but organised manner. One thing I would never give up, neither on this tour nor back at home for a day at work, was a relaxing breakfast. It has always been by far my favourite meal of every day.

I did have some concerns about today given the ascent and the distance. However, I was also excited about the challenge and pushing myself a bit to see what I was capable of. Plus I had decided to have a rest day tomorrow to enjoy being in the heart of these outstanding rocky Aravis mountains, so I could collapse in a heap for the next 36 hours if needed.

Psychologically, I had a good and speedy start with the first 15 miles being mostly downhill. I did feel like I was turning into an icicle as I whizzed along at a good pace into the freezing morning. The sun was starting to come up so I knew it wouldn't be too long before I defrosted.

Once in Samoens, I bought some food supplies for the day. According to my guidebook, Samoens is the only outdoor sports resort in France to be listed as an historic monument by the National Historic Monuments Commission. It's not surprising, this is such a pretty town with flowers tumbling out of every orifice.

A busier road into Cluses followed before commencing the ascent up the Col de la Colombiere at a lofty 1,613 metres (5,292 feet). Even though I knew I'd climbed this col last year, absolutely none of the beautiful scenery was ringing any bells at this point. The weather in the Alps during our trip last year was truly appalling with persistent, torrential deluges and even snow. Visibility had been very poor. It was a delight to pedal up in this fabulous scenery and perhaps I was genuinely seeing it for the first time.

The climb was reasonably steady and pleasant to Le Reposoir, where I stopped to eat my picnic lunch on a sunny bench. The town was so quiet, I barely saw another soul or car. I had absolutely no recollection of cycling through a town on this ascent before and started to question whether I had actually been up here previously.

I'd progressed from the Chablais region into the Aravis now. The Chablais area was a much more green and rolling area with the mountains being fully tree-clad. The Aravis was dominated by dramatic rocky peaks soaring into powder blue skies. Again, I felt the luckiest person alive to be experiencing all this by bike, particularly in such good weather when conditions in the mountains could be very changeable and unpredictable.

Onwards and upwards after lunch, steadily chugging my way up the mountain on my fully laden touring bike. As I rounded one of the corners and saw a couple of poker-straight roads ahead leading directly to the summit, the memory of cycling up this mountain came flooding back. Phew, I recognised this bit, proving that I hadn't dreamt I'd cycled up here before! What I hadn't recalled was how steep this last section becomes. Come on, road builders, this was really cruel after cycling all these miles up. I stood up, pushing down hard on the pedals and using my entire bodyweight just to get them to go round. I was absolutely not giving up at this stage. I could see and hear masses of people milling around at the top having arrived by car and motorbike. Cheats, I thought savagely.

As I summitted, I could not stop myself breaking into a massive grin at my achievement. Two ladies saw me approaching and whooped and clapped me in. I felt I deserved that! The big hairy motorbikers looked distinctly unimpressed and turned away. Nothing could dampen my euphoria at having just cycled around 17 miles uphill with all my camping and cooking gear. The views from the top were outstanding. I felt on top of the world.

Time for a treat at the café. A tea and a chocolate crepe fitted the bill and were rapidly devoured. I'm sure I could work my way through 10 of these utterly divine chocolate crepes at one sitting. In complete contrast to last year, I was able to enjoy this treat on the popular terrace outside overlooking the views. Last year, I have a very vivid memory of perusing items in their gift shop and nearly bought some oven mitts to keep my bitterly cold hands warm on the descent. Thankfully I came to my senses, realising I couldn't possible brake or change gear on the bike wearing unwieldy oven mitts on my hands, particularly on top of the three pairs of gloves I was already wearing. I did feel desperate at the time though. How lucky I felt to now be experiencing this great mountain in such incredible and gorgeous conditions.

A fabulous descent into La Grand Bornand followed, passing through some delightful floral villages. The road surface was smooth and there were few technical twists and turns.

My destination for the day was a campsite at St Jean de Sixt. The name rang a bell and I wasn't sure if I'd camped here before. A cyclist never forgets a steep climb and there was a very steep climb for about half a mile out of the town up to the campsite. How cruel! No, I definitely hadn't been here before. I should have looked up a translation for the campsite name: Le Cret, which means ridge. It would have given me a clue! The campsite was lovely with a field specifically dedicated to just tents. My tent was still tiny compared to everyone else's family mansions with multiple rooms. I felt I had everything I needed in my bijou space though.

I'd arrived in very good time around mid afternoon despite my earlier concerns regarding managing a longer day. This gave me a good opportunity to dry out the tent. Having set off so early, I'd had to pack the tent up sodden from the morning dew. I had also experienced my first shampoo explosion of the trip! Fortunately, not much had escaped as everything was well wrapped and packed up. The bit that had escaped actually made my tent smell very nice!

Having spied some washing and drying machines, I quickly showered and then threw every bit of cycling kit into the wash. Rinsing cycle clothing out in the showers does help but it just isn't the same as a full laundry wash with a good laundry powder, which I could purchase from Reception.

I cycled back into town, unencumbered by baggage, to have a quick wander and buy some fresh food for tonight's dinner. I was able to indulge in my love of fresh vegetables and stir fried onion, carrot, green pepper, courgette and tomatoes to add to my fluffy couscous for a delicious evening meal. Mixing fruit compote into natural yogurt and following this with some yummy biscuits had become my standard dessert and I loved it.

A relaxing evening followed in my now dry and sweet shampoo-smelling tent, lounging on my Thermarest chair. Two things I looked forward to every night were switching on my Blackberry to read all my new messages and reading my Kindle. My Blackberry was my lifeline to the outside world. I updated the blog on a daily basis and hugely looked forward to the messages I received from friends and family every day, be they via the blog, email or text. It felt as if everyone was with me on the journey and I enjoyed hearing "normal life" stories from home. I had been kept up to date with progress in the Tour de France and was being kept up to date with all our successes in the Olympics. I still felt a part of every day life whilst enjoying my wonderful adventure. The internet facility was also proving invaluable to locate campsites each day as well as check weather forecasts or anything else I needed, such as Google Translate, etc.

The battery life on Kindles is extraordinary. I had topped it up at Mary's and didn't need to top it up the rest of the trip. This was quite fortunate as I had not brought the plug with me, considering it unnecessary extra weight when the battery life was known to be so excellent. I had downloaded many cycle touring books and diaries and had enjoyed reading a number of those. My favourite was "Good Vibrations: Crossing Europe on a Bike Named Reggie" by Andrew Sykes. He was cycling the Eurovelo 5 from the UK to Brindisi on the south east coast of Italy. He was touring on the Ridgeback Panorama, a step up from my Ridgeback World Voyage. As Andrew was finding with his Ridgeback, my fabulous bike was proving to be a real workhorse and a trouper. He wrote of his experiences so well and it was thoroughly enjoyable following his progress on a daily basis.

The campsite was calm and peaceful with the low murmur of families chattering nearby. I slowly drifted off to sleep, looking forward immensely to my rest day tomorrow in this outstandingly beautiful region.

Chapter 23 – Sunday 5th August 2012: Rest Day in St Jean de Sixt

What a night and start to the day! After such a peaceful and unassuming evening, I was woken with a jump by violent storms battering the campsite and local area. Simultaneous roars of thunder followed vivid flashes of lightening whilst rain reverberated like popcorn off my tent. The little girl in the tent next door was crying. I didn't blame her, I felt like crying, too! This was frightening stuff and terrifyingly loud.

In my experiences in the mountains over the last few years, storms generally cleared overnight. However, storm after storm continued to plough in during the day, each one seemingly more excitable than the last. The thunderclaps sounded to bounce off the surrounding mountains. My tent porch had flooded during the night and water had got under the tent. I bailed the water out using my trusty bright pink beaker, which by now had performed a multitude of functions as a wine glass, fruit juice beaker, dessert pot and now bucket.

Life felt better after breakfast and I wrapped up warm. My new pac-a-mac from Decathlon earned its 8 euros worth dashing to the shower block and back in the deluges. I was actually incredibly grateful this was a rest day for me. Cycling in the mountains in violent storms had been a fear before setting off on the tour. I would far rather be hunkered down in my tent surrounded by other people doing the same. I had everything I needed here and could stay warm, safe and dry.

Alarmingly, my left arm was around twice its normal size and I was struggling to bend it fully due to the swelling. I'd been bitten by an evil fly yesterday and I was evidently, even to my untrained eye, having a bad reaction to it. My arm felt very hot and sometimes itchy. I slathered plenty of Savlon on to help calm it down. If the temperature deteriorated, everyone could gather round my arm for a source of heat. I at least amused myself with this thought.

Later on the morning, I felt too cramped in the tent and needed to stretch and move my body, so I decided to wander into town regardless. I had good waterproof kit so there was no need not to battle the elements on the relatively short walk.

France is mostly closed on Sundays. However, a café filled with people and atmosphere was open and I dived in to claim the last empty table and ordered a sweet and delicious hot chocolate. Noisy chatter filled the room and the one waiter dealing with everyone's food and drink orders coped admirably with the volumes of people. The windows were steamed up and I stripped off all my layers in this cosy environment.

To my amazement, a pharmacy was open for two hours today. A professional opinion on my arm would be helpful. The pharmacist didn't speak any English and my knowledge of French medical terms was basically non-existent. I rolled up my sleeve to show her the reaction to my insect bite. Her eyes popped out of her head, not a particularly reassuring start. I looked down and then so did mine, the swelling on my arm had increased in size again since walking down to the village. She firmly decided a "docteur" was needed and they would be available first thing tomorrow morning. I asked if she had anything else in the meantime. She shrugged and doubtfully produced an anti-cortisone cream. It was worth a go and it felt that I was doing something constructive. I didn't feel at all unwell so I was not unduly concerned.

The sun then came out along with the people of St Jean. I felt a special place in my heart for this lovely town and its people. It had such a wonderful and friendly vibe and atmosphere. After buying a few more supplies in the local store, another storm was threatening so I headed back to the tent and enjoyed lunch during a heavy cloudburst. My tent was coping admirably in these extreme conditions, increasing my confidence in it.

I popped to the campsite reception to ask if they knew of anyone who could look at my insect bitten arm in order that I didn't have to hang around for a doctor tomorrow. They, and all the curious onlookers, gasped in alarm and an animated debate followed in rapid-fire French, of which I understood not one word. None of them could believe the heat coming from my arm. Neither could I, I've always been such a cold person. Eventually, they all nodded in unison and an older chap gravely performed a sawing motion to chop off my arm! We all burst out laughing!

In between rainstorms during the afternoon, I took a stroll down the other side of the ridge, through pretty flower-filled hamlets. When the rain was hammering down, I snuggled into my tent, carried out some route planning, had an afternoon nap and read my Kindle. I was so glad I'd got all my clothes washed and dried yesterday. Although not exactly what I'd envisaged, this rest day had been very enjoyable and given my body a good chance to rest before the rigours of the next few days and weeks.

A friendly German family were in the neighbouring tent. The Dad had excellent English. He told me they were enjoying 6 weeks of hiking, biking and climbing in different locations around the region. He and his wife were teachers so could enjoy this lifestyle every Summer (and Easter and Christmas). Although I envy the holidays teachers receive, I applaud those who use them so well. Andrew Sykes, author of the Good Vibrations book I was reading, was a teacher and had used his Summer holidays well to fulfil an ambition. My German neighbour advised more storms were on the way throughout the evening and overnight. Great, thanks for that!

He wasn't wrong. As I started to think about cooking dinner, the distant rumbles of thunder began, the ground vibrating as it approached. I had to laugh, this reminded me so much of the scary T-Rex approaching in the Jurassic Park films! A rumble, the ground shuddered; a louder rumble, another shake of the ground, water rippling in the puddles, a flash of lightening followed by a few more and then the full strength of the storm/T-Rex was unleashed for the next 30 minutes.

Knowing I would have a window between this storm passing and the next one arriving, I chopped all my remaining veggies for another stir-fry dinner in my tent, ready to leap out and cook during that vital window.

The storm ebbed away, I jumped outside, lit the stove and started frantically cooking. The next storm was already approaching in the same Jurassic Park style. Fortunately, stir-fries are extremely quick. I knew it was possible to cook on the Trangia in a storm, I just didn't particularly fancy a rain-soaked meal. I got my lovely hot food plated up just as the thunder, rain and lightening arrived. Result! I happily ate my delicious dinner, enjoying the spectacle taking place around me from the safety of my tiny tent.

I did feel ever so slightly sad this evening. I knew my route would now head north again, most likely all the way up to Calais to catch the Bike Bus by the end of August. This meant I would be leaving the mountains where my heart belonged. I didn't have to cycle to Calais, I could continue to explore other parts of the French Alps or head further into central France and then catch a train to Calais, I hadn't yet decided. However, I knew it was pretty unlikely I would cycle up through Eastern France at any point in the future so the likelihood would be I would cycle to Calais from here.

I reminded myself how incredibly lucky I had been to cycle in the Swiss and French Alps already and what an extraordinary and brilliant journey I had enjoyed so far. I knew there would be plenty more exciting adventures to come, whatever route I took. And it would be good to broaden my horizons and explore somewhere new.

It was time to settle down to hopefully get some sleep tonight, no matter how many storms there were. I generously covered my rather misshapen insect-bitten arm with huge quantities of the cream the pharmacy had dubiously recommended before snuggling far down into my heavenly sleeping bag to hide from the bright flashes of lightening.

Chapter 24 – Monday 6th August 2012: Cycling from St Jean de Sixt to Yvoire

It was eerily silent when I awoke this morning. No rain, no thunder, no lightening, no wind, no birds singing. In fact, I wondered if I'd woken up in my bedroom at home and this whole tour had been a dream!

I unzipped the tent door and was greeted by thick, dense fog. Oh! Well, I suppose this was an improvement on yesterday's storms for a cycling day. If there had been any storms overnight, I had certainly managed to sleep through them.

I looked at my insect bitten arm in the hope that the swelling had started to recede. I was keen to get a move on today and didn't fancy hanging around for a doctor if I could help it. I still felt fully well. Although still bizarrely large and deformed, I was convinced enough that the swelling had started to go down. I'm confident I could have fried an egg on my arm, the heat was still so intense. I decided to press on with today's ride. There would be doctors in other villages should I need them. I covered my whole arm generously in my new wonder-cream and then got myself and the bike ready to head back out.

I was no longer following the route in my guidebook, which would have taken me to the shores of the beautiful Lake Annecy today. I had opted for a fairly straight route and, depending on terrain, would either make it to Bonneville or potentially all the way back up to Yvoire on Lac Leman. My map didn't have any useful contours to help me know if there were any big climbs. The word "col" didn't appear at any rate. I was really hopeful I could make it to Yvoire.

In the thick fog, I switched all my many bike and helmet lights onto flashing mode and donned my luminous yellow jacket that I'm sure can be seen from outer space. I popped into St Jean de Sixt for the last time to stock up on a few more provisions for the day. I would miss this lively little town filled with heart and chatter.

There was a faint drizzle as I set off, which became persistent rain as the day progressed. The RainLegs and my waterproof overshoes were donned.

It was downhill all the way to Bonneville. Although it was a main road, it was very quiet and I was able to admire the beauty of the deep gorge that I was cycling and freewheeling through.

Bonneville, on the other hand, was very busy with traffic. It was quite funny to think this might have been my destination for the day however I'd reached here before 10am! There was no need to pitch up so early and I felt increasingly confident that I could make it to Yvoire by the end of the day.

To get out of Bonneville, I knew I was aiming for Ayse but my map wasn't sufficiently detailed to direct me through this maze of a traffic fume-filled town. I decided to put my head down and keep pedalling determinedly until I reached the other side of the town and I would figure out what to do then. As it happened, just as I stopped to look around on the outskirts of Bonneville, I saw a sign directing me to Ayse. Awesome!

This took me onto a much quieter road and I happily pedalled along, keeping warm in the increasingly soggy conditions. Visibility was not too bad and I could enjoy my surroundings as I cycled through. I stopped a few miles further down to gobble my pain au chocolat whilst trying not to get it wet. I love pain au chocolat and this had become a daily mid-morning treat since entering France. I wanted to fuel my body well for the rigours of the road whilst still enjoying my favourite treats.

The rain grew heavier and heavier and had become a grey curtain. A cap is one of my key pieces of touring kit. It's wonderful for keeping the rain off your face at times like this, helping you feel less wet, and it also keeps the sun out of your eyes in good weather. My cap was being invaluable now.

Whilst pedalling along a waterlogged road, I saw a red double decker bus parked up ahead. It looked like a London bus. We were in the middle of nowhere. Was I hallucinating and, if so, why would I conjure up a London bus? I stopped to get a closer look and it was indeed a London bus! It was apparently going to Notting Hill. How peculiar! I took a photo for the blog and, just as I was setting back off again, I spotted what might be a café behind it. I investigated further. It was more a deli and they sold cold drinks from a fridge. I asked if they did hot tea. They didn't but were happy to make me one. I could have hugged her! There was a small marquee with a few tables and chairs outside. I took my drenched outer clothes off and soon started to shake with cold despite the warmth of the sweet tea seeping through my bones. It was best not to hang around for too long and to keep making progress towards Yvoire.

I warmed as I started to climb steadily uphill and opted to eat lunch in a large stone built bus shelter that was about half the size of my entire flat. Even though it was simply a bus shelter, it seemed to ooze character. There was a convenient bench to sit on running alongside an entire wall plus it was well protected from the elements. If only it were heated, too! It wouldn't be my normal choice for a lunch stop but today it fitted the bill just perfectly.

I was apparently heading up the Col du Perret, which wasn't marked on my map and turned out to be just shy of 1,000 metres (3,280 feet). I was quite close to Saint Cergues again although Mary, Rene and Max were still back in England at this time.

As I continued my steady climb in the incessant rain, a white van ahead came to a stop and a guy ran out towards me in completely bare feet, holding something in his hands. It was difficult to see properly with the rain coming down and then I laughed when I realised he was offering me a banana in one hand and a Snickers bar in the other! He was Dutch and he and the female driver, who had also joined us and was at least wearing some shoes, were driving the support van for a Dutch cycle touring company. We spoke in French until he realised I was English and then perfect fluent English flowed from both of them. The Dutch are amazing for their English skills. They offered me anything I needed from the van. I gratefully accepted the banana and topped up my water bottles, although I wasn't drinking much of the cold stuff today. They cheered me up by telling me the weather was forecast to pick up from tomorrow for the rest of the week. They told me they thought I was amazing for touring on my own and carrying all my own kit, particularly in these conditions. I was really flattered. Despite the cold, they'd warmed me up with their friendliness, kindness and slight zaniness in their approach. Between them and the lady at the deli with the red London bus making me a hot cup of tea, they'd all really made my day on what was otherwise a murky, wet and grey Monday.

I happily continued to pedal along through the rain in the rolling green hills towards Yvoire. As I approached the village, it started to absolutely bucket it down. Rivers of water poured through my helmet, down my arms and off my legs. There is not really anything you can do when so wet other than continue regardless. Cycling in such dramatic conditions usually makes me laugh at the insanity of it all. I was doing the same today. Thankfully, I remained toasty warm inside my good quality cycling kit.

I felt thoroughly bedraggled upon reaching Yvoire and water continued to pour off me as I stood waiting at the campsite reception. They didn't seem to notice the puddle forming round me and treated me the same as all the other well dressed, civilised people milling around. I appreciated that. The campsite was almost full to bursting but they found me a nice little pitch at the far end of a field attached to the campsite. It seemed to be true that French campsites would always find a spot for cycle-campers.

After all that rain all day, the weather finally started to improve, enabling me to erect the tent in dry conditions for which I was grateful. There were no shops nearby and I was directed to the nearby village of Messery, 2-3 kilometres away. I decided to cycle there quickly whilst leaving the tent to dry out as much as possible. The small supermarket there was wonderful. I wished, not for the first time, that I could carry more food. It was a shame not to be able to stock up on more whilst it was available.

Back at the campsite, I had a feeling the toilets would be of the squat variety, given those in the nearby village of Yvoire were. I was proved correct and just did my best to get on with it. It's all part of the adventure, Andi! The showers were equally peculiar with a chain to pull to release water. It had been the same system in St Jean de Sixt and I'd experienced it at one campsite on the Alps trip last year. I was extremely thankful that the water in the showers was superbly hot and I felt restored in no time.

The sun came out in the evening, allowing all my cycle clothes and my towel to dry. I usually treated myself to a meal out every 3 to 4 evenings. I was due a meal out tonight and had been looking forward to doing so in the stunningly beautiful setting of Yvoire. However, I just really wanted to eat a huge bowl of hot, steaming pasta and the sooner, the better. I made a lovely pasta dish with plenty of fresh vegetables in a deliciously warming tomato sauce. I then followed this with not one but two small pots of tiramisu from the supermarket. Well, the 2nd one might have gone off by tomorrow night….! I sipped my mug of hot green tea allowing the warmth of the evening sun to envelope and relax me.

What a fabulous day with some unexpected treats! I'd cycled 61 miles at a more respectable 11mph average thanks to easier terrain and despite one small col. Tomorrow, I would be catching a ferry across the lake and starting my journey up through the Jura Mountains. I had a number of possible routes in mind and would make it up as I went along. I did want to cycle in the Jura, however I was also quite keen to cycle to the Lac de Neuchatel. It looked like I could do a bit of both.

I fell into a deep, relaxed and happy sleep.

Chapter 25 – Tuesday 7th August 2012: Cycling from Yvoire to Cossonay

What a gorgeous night's sleep last night. My priority straight after breakfast was cycling the few kilometres back to Messery to get today's fresh supplies. Other than the little Casino supermarket there, I'd seen a bakery a bit further down the road and wanted to ensure I had my trusty pain au chocolat and baguette with me for the day ahead. Who knew what was in store on the northern shores of Lac Leman. Would it be similar to the north or south of the river divide in London?! Was it considered better to live north of the lake or south? I would find out today.

The cost of the ferry crossing from Yvoire to Nyon seemed a bit steep at 12 euros 20 for me and a further 7 euros for my bike. The crossing was only 20 minutes. There was no escaping the sheer beauty of the lake and surrounding shoreline, it was absolutely breathtaking. I didn't know which direction to look in first – the Alps, the Jura, the historic villages, the glimpse of the famous Jet (the enormous water fountain in Geneva). There was a lot to see in 20 minutes and it felt a privilege to sail across this fabulous lake. I also just about managed to explain to a curious and very chic French lady about my bicycle tour. She didn't seem remotely put off by me struggling to find the words, she seemed to understand and then would ask more questions. We must have looked quite a spectacle – her oozing Parisian chic and style and all in black, me in my bright, multi-coloured cycling apparel.

A cup of tea was obviously my first priority when we disembarked in Nyon. I needed to check the map and decide where to go from here. I arrived in sparkling sunshine and was looking forward to the day ahead. I was now back on Swiss territory and back to my Swiss Francs purse. Given the main road seemed pretty quiet, I cycled along the shores of the lake towards Rolle. I was successful in locating regional Route 63 here, which took me a short way up into the hills and away from the shoreline.

The views were exceptionally pretty across the lake and looking out towards the Alpine backdrop that I'd recently cycled through. I was now pedalling initially through verdant vineyards and then latterly across large swathes of fields where haymaking activities were taking place, in fabulous sunshine, feeling ridiculously happy and free. The French influence seemed very strong in this part of Switzerland although I was delighted to see the return of the Swiss water fountains where plentiful cool, fresh drinking water was freely available.

As I pedalled onwards, I could see the seemingly enormous urban sprawl of Lausanne even though I was heading northwards and away from the lake. Regional Route 63 joined National Route 5 as I continued the journey north. I was intending to stay on Route 5 until I reached the Lac de Neuchatel and then decide whether to continue along it or head upwards to Route 7, which was the route through the Jura. I couldn't see any campsites noted on my map so kept my eyes peeled for guest-house accommodation as well.

Fortunately, as I cycled through Cossonay, I spotted a sign for a campsite. This seemed the most unlikely place. It looked as if I was in a social housing estate and, although slightly more run down than other areas I'd experienced across Switzerland, it was extremely tidy and well looked after. The sign proved to be correct and I descended down a scarily steep hill into a very lively and fun-filled holiday camp.

After locating the chap in charge, he found me a spot amidst the caravans for my little tent and charged me a very reasonable CHF10. Again, there were no others camping in tents at this "campsite". The atmosphere was fantastic with hundreds of children making good use of the extensive swimming pool and diving board facilities.

I popped back up to the Co-op I'd seen back in the village and treated myself to some very lovely food for later this evening. After showering, I relaxed in the site bar with a glass of chilled white wine, watching the hive of activity in the swimming pool and on the surrounding terraces. Wine seems to be the only commodity in Switzerland that doesn't cost the earth. A glass here is much cheaper than the UK, typically costing between £1-£3.

I'd cheated this evening and bought a ready-made pasta and roasted vegetable meal that simply needed heating. I added my remaining fresh vegetables and enjoyed this all with a refreshing salad with a balsamic vinegar dressing and some crusty bread. Camp food doesn't have to be pot noodles! Yoghurt, fruit compote and biscuits followed and, as I sat sipping my green tea, I thought that this was, indeed, the life.

Consulting my map, I was pleased I had chosen to do a hybrid route up to Basel, mixing Route 5 with Route 7. The Swiss cycling system, again, was making the planning and the cycling very straightforward. I knew the routes had been designed to pass through the most scenic areas of their special country and along the quietest roads. As well as having designated national, regional and local cycling routes, the Swiss have also devised the same for mountain biking, hiking and roller-blading. All of these routes were recorded on the Swiss Activity Map I had purchased in Thun. All of these routes were also clearly signposted. What a super-organised nation!

With the earliest ferry crossing this morning being mid-morning, my mileage today reached just 34 miles. I felt a bit lazy doing such low mileages compared to previous tours, particularly when I hadn't climbed any mountains today. I reminded myself this trip was about experiencing the places and the people and enjoying myself rather than simply focusing on putting my head down and covering longer distances. So many people were writing supportively on the blog about how proud they were of me and how amazing they thought I was doing what I was doing. I genuinely didn't feel very amazing, especially with such easy-life mileages, and I was slightly baffled and humbled by what they were saying. I certainly needed and appreciated everyone's support and loved them all for what they were saying. The trip would have had a completely different feel without everyone's tremendous and ongoing encouragement.

I needed to get back out of analysis mode and just go with the flow. I was still achieving something very different to what I'd done before and I was proud of myself for having a go. Keep enjoying it!

Chapter 26 – Wednesday 8th August 2012: Cycling from Cossonay to St Croix

After a fairly chilly night, the sun rose to dry my tent beautifully before I packed it away this morning. It also warmed me up as I pedalled away with the aim of reaching the Lac de Neuchatel.

Route 5 was very different from the Swiss and French Alpine regions I'd been cycling in. It was very pleasant cycling along gently rolling terrain, usually surrounded by vast fields with villages visible in the distance and very often along railway lines. I was really starting to think that the railways were built before the rest of Switzerland! They were so well placed and connected the entire country seemingly effortlessly. There were a few more cyclists along this route although, as I had experienced in the Swiss Alps, fellow cyclists don't tend to acknowledge you at all. I tried to stop thinking this was really rude, it was simply their culture and their way. I was probably considered rude and shocking to them by waving a cheery hello.

I enjoyed a very special moment today. Cycling along an empty road, I stopped on a ridge to have a good look at the surrounding scenery and gasped in joy and amazement. Above the hazy clouds were the rocky peaks of the Alps. It looked surreal and completely magical. Not only that, majestically rising above them all was the magnificent Mont Blanc, elusive my entire tour so far, its snow-capped peak shimmering in the distance. I nearly whooped with delight, I was so happy to finally see the highest mountain in the Alps. I took a number of photos and then took another moment to take it all in. Wow!

Arriving into Yverdon-les-Bains on the shores of Lac de Neuchatel was another highlight. A timeless, historic and stunningly beautiful small town, I stopped for a cup of tea in the warm sunshine to admire the splendour and simplicity of the character buildings. On the approach into Yverdon, the main road feeding this town was built on giant stilts, thereby not impacting the fields of corn being grown in the valley below. It was great to see a skateboarding park and activity area had been built underneath the main road, alongside my cycle route, making superb use of this otherwise dead space. A number of families and teenagers were here honing their skills.

I was keen to get to the lake itself and could just see a glimpse of the sparkling turquoise waters from the town. I bade farewell to Route 5 at this point and picked up regional routes 22 and 50, which, according to my map, appeared to hug the edge of the entire northern shoreline to Neuchatel. It seemed to take a while to cycle to the actual lake from the town as the route deviated out of town first and I was getting impatient to see the lake properly!

I didn't have too long to wait long before the dazzling lake came into view. My heart sang as I cycled along this spectacular lake in fabulous sunshine. I was literally bursting with happiness. I stopped for lunch on some picnic tables in a small village called Grandson, admiring the beauty of the lake and surrounding pretty flower-filled parkland as I ate.

I continued along the railway line, the route generally now hiding the lake from view. Through forested areas and back cycling through the vast expanses of fields. Although it was very pretty, I realised I was starting to find the route a little bit boring. I felt bad for thinking this, I would normally be cooped up in an office on this working day rather than cycling freely in lovely countryside in superb weather. However, I knew I was missing the hills and mountains. This is where my heart truly belongs. I had been cycling in the valley with the Jura Mountains tempting me on my left hand side for mile after mile. I knew this is now where I wanted to be.

Arriving in a village with no signposts, as can often be the case in the usually efficient Switzerland, I saw a local cycle route signpost showing the way to a village called Champagne, which I could see on my map. It was heading in roughly the right direction for the Jura, so up the steep climb I went. The route then literally took me completely back on myself, although I was at least heading upwards and into the forested sub-alpine region of the Jura mountains now.

My levels of happiness soared as I pedalled gradually upwards on empty smooth roads, the Alps and the Lac de Neuchatel now clearly visible on my left and the green of the Jura on my right. I was aiming to ultimately join national Route 7, which would take me safely all the way to Basel in the north of Switzerland where I could then cross the border into France and continue my journey northwards to Calais.

As the day progressed, the roads became narrower and I cycled through tiny hamlets consisting of a few houses where there were no signs of life. No cars, no people, no shops, no facilities. Thankfully, there were still much needed water fountains as I passed through.

Upon reaching a busier and more mainstream road, it did not look far on my map before I would reach Route 7. But, oh, the climb! This road went onwards and upwards for 10 hot, sweaty, leg-burning, lung-busting miles until arriving in the town of St Croix. There was no doubting I was now firmly in the Jura mountains. I knew that I didn't have much left in my legs and set about searching for a campsite. The tourist office had just closed and there were no campsites shown on my map. It was already after 5pm whereas I would normally aim to stop around 3pm.

I wandered up the main street and spotted a guest house sign. I absolutely dreaded how much a hotel might cost for the night in Switzerland. To allay this fear, it seems such establishments are obliged to publish their rates outside the building and I couldn't believe that this guesthouse was only CHF30. If they had any spare rooms, I would bite their hands off for it!

Fortunately for me, they did have a spare room that night and they had a garage to safely lock my trusty steed in. My room was spacious but cold and smelt of damp. There was broken glass in the window. I opened the window to let in some fresh air. Despite some of these unexpected conditions, I very much appreciated being here. There was a sink in the corner of my room as the bathroom was shared with the other guests. The bedlinen was spotlessly clean and towels were provided.

As always, a hot and powerful shower restored my soul and I went for a gentle walk around this small town in the warm evening sunshine afterwards. My guesthouse offered food and, in the absence of any other open restaurants, I ate my dinner there. A chilled glass of dry white wine relaxed me further as I tucked into another of my favourite meals, a delicious homemade vegetable pizza with a fresh green salad.

I'd cycled 45 miles today and was glad to now be high in the Jura Mountains. I was happy with the convoluted route I'd taken to get here. I wouldn't have seen Mont Blanc towering in the distance nor would I have experienced the timeless beauty of Yverdon-les-Bains and the striking Lac de Neuchatel if I'd simply travelled along Route 7 from Nyon on Lac Leman. I wouldn't have missed any of those sights and experiences for the world.

I knew I had a hilly start in the morning and therefore opted for a reasonably early night.

Chapter 27 – Thursday 9th August 2012: Cycling from St Croix to La Chaux de Fonds

Continental breakfasts can really differ from place to place and, at this hotel, a very simple breakfast was offered. A small glass of juice, some bread, butter and jam, a croissant and a mug of tea. That did little to satisfy my raging cycling hunger so I ran across the road to buy some milk from the supermarket and indulged in a big and delicious bowl of my own muesli, too.

Having also stocked up on supplies whilst at the supermarket opposite the hotel, I headed onwards and upwards, now joining Route 7.

Once off the main road, the climbs in the Jura are steep. I pined for the comparatively easier gradients of Alpine France. The sun was baking hot although I was well shaded by the heavily forested hills. Despite this relief, it also meant there were not really any views other than lots of trees, trees and more trees. It was hard to keep the bike upright as I slowly toiled uphill whilst trying to fend off more evil biting flies that had caused the bad reaction on my arm a few days ago. One of the blighters got me on my left calf. I'd get my wonder-cream smothered on that as soon as possible, once I didn't have rivers of sweat pouring down my legs. My knees were starting to hurt carrying all this weight up prolonged steep ascents.

It was always worth it when I stopped to eat my morning pain au chocolat, wherever I was. Although a sweaty mess, I still absolutely loved the sun and the heat. At home, all year I'd had to pile on multiple layers of clothing to stay warm and dry. Here, I was in shorts and a vest top. Simple! Unfortunately, this provided plentiful exposed flesh for those evil flies.

I stopped for a cup of tea in Fleurier. The service was surly, almost verging on rude. I felt slightly offended but maintained my cheery demeanour. The tea was lovely and I'd needed the break.

Having not seen many cycle tourists at all so far, I was delighted to see some approaching from the other direction. I should have known better, I was completely blanked as they cycled past. This is so different to our culture and I still couldn't get my head around the lack of friendliness. I reminded myself once again that this is their way and I'm in their country, I need to adopt their approach. For my last few days in Switzerland, I merely raised my hand in acknowledgement rather than smiling or saying hello. This elicited a better response and I felt much happier that there had been some connection between Swiss cyclists and me.

The roads became bigger and busier as I approached La Chaux de Fonds. Although on a cycle path, being alongside 2 and 3 lanes of fast heavy traffic was quite nerve jangling. I knew there were some campsites here and followed the first sign I saw, eager to get off these carriageways.

Of course, as is always the case when your legs are super-tired, there was a short but extremely steep climb to haul the bike and me up to reach the campsite. But what an oasis of peace and calm when I emerged in this sanctuary surrounded by trees, which seemed to completely drown out the noise of the traffic below. It looked and felt as if you were in a completely rural setting.

After checking in, I discovered the only nearby shops were several miles along the carriageways into la Chaux de Fonds itself. I decided to see what rations I had in my panniers. I knew I was out of fresh stuff but had some packets of food that simply needed heating up with water. If I'd bought any fresh food in the morning, it certainly wouldn't have survived in today's heat anyway.

I appreciate this won't appeal to everyone, but I had a tofu, tomato and basil ravioli. This I enjoyed with some leftover bread from lunch. Described as a meal for one, it certainly wasn't sufficient for a hungry cyclist so I delved back into my panniers. A-ha! My good friend, Adele, had very kindly given me an incredibly thoughtful gift before I embarked on the tour which she told me to keep at the bottom of my panniers for an emergency. This constituted an emergency, there was nowhere else to buy food and I was still hungry. A chocolate pudding with hot chocolate sauce! Oh my word! I excitedly heated up this delectable pudding and savoured every single rich and gooey, chocolatey mouthful. What heaven! In my head, I thanked Adele over and over again for coming to my rescue tonight. I sat back contentedly in my Thermarest chair with my mug of green tea, enjoying the relaxed chatter of nearby fellow campers.

A lovely lady with a great grasp of English came over to talk to me. She was originally from Basel, a city of which she was very proud, and now lived in Zurich. She was so happy to hear I was cycling to her beloved Basel and wished me well. She restored my faith in the Swiss on a day where I hadn't, until now, experienced their friendliest side. They are generally very lovely people, they just don't express it as outwardly as we do.

I'd completed 41 miles today. I scoured the map for campsites to plan my new few days to Basel. It looked like I needed to cycle two relatively short days to ensure I would have sites to stay at. There were certainly less campsites in this area compared to the Swiss and French Alps, so more careful planning was required. I was happy to stay in accommodation maybe up to once a week if I needed but had a strong preference for camping as much as possible.

The temperature was dropping quite sharply in the evening after the heat of the day. My left calf had ballooned from the insect bite this morning and I therefore applied plenty of wonder-cream that had helped my arm so much a few days ago. It was then time to snuggle down into my luxurious sleeping bag and lavender scented travel pillow for another blissful night's sleep.

Chapter 28 – Friday 10th August 2012: Cycling from La Chaux de Fonds to St Ursanne

Today's cycling was considerably more enjoyable out of the densely forested, and occasionally, oppressive region of the Jura Mountains. I was cycling through open spaces, in the sunshine and through many farming areas that were hard at work hay-making.

Although I'd eaten a good breakfast, having a smaller meal last night was rapidly catching up with me. I hadn't passed any shops or villages for many miles and I was completely out of biscuits. This hadn't been an issue so far all tour but it was becoming apparent that the Jura was less populated and there were therefore less facilities (other than if I fancied a hair-raising cycle along a 3 lane carriageway into the nearest town or city).

I was relieved to see a sign ahead that indicated a restaurant in the middle of nowhere. It was called "Little Ranch" and the board showed it to be open as I approached. I saw a couple already enjoying a coffee on the terrace overlooking spectacular views. Sweet relief! I happily sat down and ordered a cup of tea, asking what they had to eat. Nothing! There had been no deliveries yet. I asked if there were any shops with provisions nearby. A lot of head shaking followed from the proprietor and the couple as they tried to ascertain just how far it was to the nearest store. Oh dear. I said I was very hungry but the tea would help.

When the proprietor had gone inside to make my drink, the couple sat nearby explained that the restaurant wasn't actually open until lunchtime. Oops! I couldn't believe the chap was still happy to make me a drink, how lovely. The couple were either friends or family and had stopped by for a cuppa and catch up. As they knew I was hungry, they gave me the mini chocolates that had accompanied their drinks! I was so touched. The proprietor also brought out his last two mini chocolates with my tea.

The couple left and I conversed with the proprietor as best I could, saying what a stunningly beautiful place to live and he must love it here. He was so pleased to meet an "English lady" cycling through his incredible country and was so impressed by my trip that he refused payment for the tea. I insisted he take the money, particularly given he was actually closed and yet had still served me, but he wanted to give me a gift for the tour. Overwhelmed, I thanked him profusely. I will never forget that lovely man for making such a positive difference to my day.

Food proved to be very difficult to find today. I deviated off route when in the village of Les Breuloux, thinking they must have some shops here. Unfortunately, this did involve cycling down a steep hill, which meant I would have to cycle back up it again to re-join the route. I found a butcher's shop. Not particularly helpful for a vegetarian. There was a library, a school, a church, some offices. For heaven's sake, there must be a bakery or general stores somewhere.

I eventually located a general stores, tucked away at the bottom of the hill. It wasn't a brilliant store and the bakery section was miniscule and very poor. It didn't even have any bread! It cost seemingly the equivalent of a mortgage to buy a few yoghurts, fruit, veg, cheese, biscuits and fruit compote. Blimey. How does anyone afford to live here?

I devoured much of the food on a bench outside the store. I really was incredibly hungry and it wasn't even lunchtime. Perhaps the thought of neither having any food on me nor knowing where I could buy any probably made me feel hungrier than I actually was. It did, however, feel very real at the time.

I needed to find somewhere with a decent store to stock up properly. Looking at the map, I would be passing Saignelegier, which looked to be a town of reasonable size.

However, the cycle route once again took you away from the town. I needed to go into the town. I knew I could make it back to the route if I deviated for a short time.

The town was a few miles off route. The famous annual horse fair was arriving this weekend so much of the town was cordoned off with alternative routes in place. Undeterred, I walked the bike through all the now pedestrianised areas and decided to stop for a proper lunch at a café or restaurant rather than having my usual picnic lunch.

I sat in a sunny spot on a small patch of outside space at one restaurant. They had nothing vegetarian but were happy to do me bread, chips and salad. I needed the carbo-loading. Whilst waiting for the food, I enjoyed the spectacle and lively atmosphere taking place around me. This horse fair was the biggest event of the year in this region. I felt privileged to be a part of the excitement as the final arrangements were being made. I wouldn't have known anything about this had I not been so hungry and stayed on the route.

I've never seen such an enormous plate of chips! I wolfed them down along with the crusty bread and lovely refreshing salad, feeling fully sated. Happy, happy days!

As I then washed this feast down with a cup of tea, a bloke came out onto the terrace for a cigarette. When he discovered I was English, he became very animated and spoke fluent English from then on. He was an engineer and had worked often in England. He loved my home county of Yorkshire, saying the best things to come out of Yorkshire were the brass bands (very good) and Yorkshire Building Society…. (I'm sorry??). I was slightly baffled but that was his opinion. He was hugely enthusiastic, he made me laugh and I learnt a lot about him before saying cheerio. He definitely didn't fit the usual profile of the Swiss people I'd met.

I stocked up as much as my bulging panniers would allow at the local Co-op before re-joining Route 7. I was heading for St Brais where a campsite was marked on my map. It didn't look too much further and it definitely didn't look like there would be any shops or facilities. I was comforted that I'd stocked up so well in Saignelegier.

I cycled through St Brais, keeping my eyes peeled for the campsite. I realised I had then cycled all the way through St Brais and had not spotted any sign for a campsite. Oh dear. My heart sinking, I cycled back up the hill through the village to check again. There was definitely no sign of a campsite anywhere.

Luckily, I could see two people working on their front garden further down the road. I very rarely saw people as I cycled through villages here. I cycled up and asked them about the location of the campsite. At first, they continued gardening and seemed to ignore me. I tried again. With a sigh, the man came over to see what I wanted. He and the woman agreed there was no campsite in St Brais and hadn't been as long as they could remember, regardless of what my map was showing. However, they did know of a campsite in St Ursanne around 10 kilometres away. After the initial shaky start, the guy really got into the conversation, thinking of all the possibilities and then recommending the best route to this campsite. He then became even more excitable, talking about how the Tour de France had cycled past his home on this very road and that Bradley Wiggins had won and he was English and I was English so I must be great!! I silently thanked Bradley Wiggins for helping me open up this conversation into a very helpful and friendly dialogue.

After bading farewell to this now lovely family, I followed his instructions which involved a climb of a couple of miles and then one of the longest descents I could remember doing in a while. I sincerely hoped I didn't need to cycle back up here tomorrow, the gradients were steep.

Catching my breath at the bottom of the decent by the exceptionally pretty Doubs river, I spotted signs for the campsite he had referred to and, with relief, pulled into it. Reception wasn't open until 5pm. I had an hour to go. The sign invited me to pitch up on a thin strip of grass the other side of a wire fence separating campers from the hostel and activity area. Despite the very limited area, the grass was lovely and springy and I didn't need much space for my little tent anyway.

The welcome was very friendly when Reception opened and I felt very much at home here in this lovely basin of the Doubs valley. The shower was fabulous and I relaxed over a divine glass of white wine whilst contemplating my next steps. Quite honestly, I could do with another rest day and I knew I would be happy to stay here for a day off. I wanted to make the most of this extraordinary blue sky and hot sunshine before heading north into most likely cooler, cloudier and wetter conditions.

I thoroughly enjoyed my camp-cooked dinner of spinach and ricotta tortellini in a pesto sauce with fresh broccoli and courgette. My favourite natural yoghurt with a fruit compote followed, into which I chopped my last fresh apricot, and I then indulged in some biscuits with my green tea. I truly felt fully re-fuelled and content.

I went for a late evening stroll into the nearby town of St Ursanne, which was an unexpected charming medieval treat. I did clock the small Co-op as I entered under the stone archway of the castle walls into the streets of the town and its higgledy-piggledy historic buildings with pastel shutters. It was indescribably pretty and very tranquil.

Darkness was falling and I wanted to return before any other annoying insects decided to bite me. My left calf was still one and half times it's normal size from the latest bite but I was confident the swelling would go down with continued use of the wonder-cream.

Yes, I would definitely spend tomorrow exploring the area here and enjoying what could be the last of my sunshine and warmth. Nestling down into my cosy sleeping bag, I drifted happily into a deep, contented sleep.

Chapter 29 – Saturday 11ᵗʰ August 2012: Rest Day in St Ursanne, Switzerland

I've never been any good at having a lay-in, despite my best intentions. The morning was chilly and I wanted to stay snuggled inside my warm sleeping bag but I was also keen to get on with my day. There was food to buy, laundry to do, the bike to check, routes to plan, sightseeing to enjoy. Invariably there was very little actual resting on a rest day. My golden rule was simply not to cycle. My body always benefited from a break from the saddle.

After a hearty and enjoyable breakfast, I ensured the laundry was on as early as possible. The washing machine here had an excellent spin so my clothes emerged mostly dry. They had plenty of washing lines for me to hang the clothes out on. The lines turned out to be for the bedding and towels laundry from the hostel but they didn't seem to have any issue with my small number of clothes taking up some space for a while.

I stocked up on plenty of supplies from the Co-op in the nearby St Ursanne town. Fortunately, I was able to keep lots of food fresh in the communal fridge at the campsite. Tomorrow was Sunday and everywhere would be shut, I was determined to have everything I needed.

I decided as I rapidly spent my dwindling Swiss Francs throughout the day that I wanted to get out of Switzerland and back into France as soon as possible, tomorrow if feasible. The high prices of everything and the lack of facilities en route were really starting to get to me. On Route 4 across the Swiss Alps, the route passed through many villages and shops making obtaining supplies quite easy. This Route 7 seemed to actively take you away from any places of habitation. I was also missing the great friendliness of French cyclists whilst on the road. I felt snubbed or shunned when fellow cyclists went past without acknowledgment. Heading into France earlier would also save me from cycling back into German speaking Switzerland where my knowledge of this language was more limited. As a final point, I knew I had no real desire to cycle into a city the size of Basel. If I could avoid that now, I would.

I packed up a picnic in my nifty foldaway rucksack, took my map and set off walking down the river Doubs to find a nice shady spot for lunch and to consider my options. It was entertaining watching a number of families who were shrieking with laughter as they attempted to canoe along the river. Family life seemed very important to the holidaying Swiss and it was wonderful to watch.

Upon consulting the map, it appeared that I could continue along Route 7 for a short while and would then be able to pick up regional route 64 which would take me to the border with France. I would then have a few short miles to cycle to Joncherey and its campsite. I double checked the campsite in Joncherey existed using the internet connection on my Blackberry to be sure.

The Doubs valley and the river were stunningly beautiful and I spent some time taking in the scenery and the sunshine. I really liked this place. I wondered how harsh it must be in the Winter here. It was difficult to imagine whilst being surrounded by the sights, sounds and smells of Summer.

A long walk really helped loosen off my legs although my swollen left calf throbbed from the insect bite. The swelling was starting to reduce. As well as feeling extremely hot, the whole area felt pretty badly bruised and tender. I needed to get away from these evil biting flies. I hadn't experienced such bad reactions to any bites or stings in the past.

There didn't appear to be any issues with the bike. It could do with the tyres pumping up properly if I passed a bike shop but they weren't too bad. All the gears and brakes were working. The chain was always my main concern and I regularly cleaned and oiled it. It was considerably easier to look after the chain in such dry conditions. It would have been much tougher if it had persistently rained. Overall, my bike looked robust and happy!

Knowing I would leave Switzerland tomorrow, I felt free to spend more of my Swiss francs. I couldn't believe that it would be the first time on the entire trip that I would be indulging in some Swiss ice-cream. I hadn't been living! This ice-cream was exceptional and almost worth the ridiculously high price tag. It felt 100 degrees outside so it was a wonderfully refreshing treat. St Ursanne was also breaking impressive records for my most expensive cup of tea in a café and the most expensive small glass of pink grapefruit juice at a bar. I was thankful the wine was so cheap back at the campsite.

As I returned to my tent to cook dinner in the evening, a couple were busy setting their tent up near to mine. Were those English voices I heard? Yes! They were Australian, in fact, and were approaching the end of their two year rail tour around the world. Wow, that put my tiny 6 week trip into perspective! They occasionally got homesick. I know I already did in my short time in Europe so far. Seeing so many families together made me miss my family and friends and I wanted to share many sights and experiences with them. However, I was fortunate to be able to stay in touch via the blog, text and email and was enjoying travelling solo.

They were a bit stuck for food as the Co-op was now shut until Monday. The campsite owner had provided them with a few bits and pieces and I donated my remaining veggies. They wouldn't keep in this heat tomorrow anyway so they were doing me a favour.

I was excited at the thought of cycling out of Switzerland and back into France tomorrow. I had planned the next couple of day's cycling, which would take me to the edge of my map. I needed to source some local maps to continue on the best routes possible as I started to make my way towards Calais.

I was admittedly also quite nervous about this next stage. For the last 3 weeks, I had been on recognised routes following signposts or a guidebook. Now, I was completely on my own. I knew I did want to try to cycle all the way to Calais and I had a rough idea of how to make my way there using my map of France. I now needed to buy some local maps to ascertain the detail of how to make it bit by bit across the country.

I was still so reluctant to leave the fabulous warmth and sunshine behind. Why couldn't I have opted to cycle southwards? I had been so lucky to experience the fabulous weather I had overall and I had plenty of good kit for worsening conditions. I couldn't envisage cycling up eastern France another time so this was my opportunity to see lots of different places. I would most likely be taking in the Vosges Mountains and the Champagne region of France. I'd seen a photo on the internet of the Grand Ballon, the highest peak in the Vosges mountain range, and this had given me the inspiration to visit this area. The reason for considering visiting the Champagne area needs no explanation!

Andrew Sykes book that I was currently reading on the Kindle had been very helpful with my route planning. He had chosen a very flat route across the borders with Belgium, Luxembourg and Germany to reach Basel. The chances were I would prefer a slower, hillier route to keep my interest. I knew the area around Calais was very flat having cycled around there before. It would be nice to finish the tour with some easy spinning along quiet country lanes to work off any stiffness.

Just another 3 weeks to go!

Chapter 30 – Sunday 12th August 2012: Cycling from St Ursanne, Switzerland to Joncherey, France

Excited about cycling back into France today, I slept well and enjoyed my usual fabulous and hearty breakfast before departing for another country.

My first 3 miles took a whopping 45 minutes as I climbed up and over a mini-mountain; my next 3 miles then took a speedy 10 minutes as I descended it. The initial climb certainly warmed me up and, although on a main road, there were almost no cars this peaceful Sunday morning so I had the lovely smooth tarmac surface to myself.

I passed a shop that was open by a petrol station where I bought a pain au chocolat for later that morning. I wasn't in the most scenic place when I ate it overlooking a motorway.

As I seemed to be making excellent progress along the considerably flatter terrain of today's ride, I decided to deviate into Porrentruy. This town had hosted a stage of the Tour de France a few weeks ago. There were still banners everywhere proudly displaying this fact. The cityscape was dominated by the impressive medieval castle as I cycled into the old town. Although it was Sunday, a few cafes were open. I needed to get rid of some more Swiss Francs coins and managed this perfectly at the station café, the only place currently basking in sunshine. I had not a single cent left in change by the time I left. I still had some Swiss notes which I could convert to euros in France. I also remembered to post my postcards with Swiss stamps on before leaving the country.

I had a few false starts leaving Porrentruy, the downside of not having sufficiently detailed town maps. I had made the classic mistake of "making" my map fit the situation as I merrily pedalled on a cycle path along the railway line before acknowledging that my map didn't show the route alongside a railway line, even though everything else seemed to be in the right place. I needed to head all the way back to where I started and then continue in completely the opposite direction. Detours aren't too bad when the weather is good, your legs are fresh and the terrain flat. Admittedly, it is better not to detour in the first place though.

I cycled through endless delightful villages (with no shops) in Switzerland all morning. Each village seemed to be working hard to outdo the other in terms of exceptional prettiness. This was the best way I could have exited Switzerland. The pedalling had been enjoyable and mostly easy. It was sunny, there was no wind, it was delightfully tranquil. I had located route 64 without issue in Cornol. I left this country thinking only good things.

I was absolutely ecstatic when I cycled across the border back into France and broke into a huge grin. There was a large board announcing the fact that you were now in France, although it seemed bizarre to be placed on such a small and quiet country road in the middle of nowhere. I took a photo of the board to mark the occasion and continued pedalling feeling relieved and so glad to be back in this friendlier, cheaper country.

I reached Joncherey and the campsite earlier than I thought. It was only lunchtime. I considered continuing but the next campsite looked quite far away and I wasn't in a rush. Even with my unexpected detour in Porrentruy, I had only just clocked 31 miles. There was no problem checking in so early. The couple and their dog who looked after this campsite were so lovely. This was a beautiful site with fabulous views at the top of the hill (note again: campsites are always at the top of a hill) with lots of lovely grassy areas and mature trees providing shade and creating a pleasant light breeze. The Jura Mountains were still visible in the distance. It was fun seeing where I had cycled from today.

I found a nice spot to pitch my tent. The tent had been packed up sopping wet from the dew this morning so I pitched it and let it dry out whilst eating my picnic. Lunch consisted of some quite stale and chewy bread left over from yesterday, some reasonably sweaty cheese and a warm plump tomato. I hadn't found anywhere to buy any provisions today.

I asked at reception where the nearest store or restaurant might be for tonight. The camp owner looked at me in surprise. "Madam, it is Sunday. France is closed" he stated matter of factly. Oh dear. He saw my crestfallen face and immediately offered to collect a pizza for me tonight from a restaurant in a nearby village. Wow, what generosity and kindness. I very gratefully accepted his offer.

I spent the afternoon walking the few miles into the village of Joncherey and back, keen to see where I would be able to buy supplies tomorrow morning. The only village shop was closed for the entire month as the owners took their Summer holiday. I had also walked to the industrial outskirts of the nearby town of Delle. They had some supermarkets, which would be open in the morning. I always felt much happier if I knew where I could get some food. Anyone would have thought I was cycling through the middle of an uninhabited desert rather than the very Western and civilised countries of Switzerland and France!

My feet were quite sore from all the walking on blisteringly hot pavements by the time I returned to the campsite and I was happy to then relax. I ordered a very tasty veggie pizza with a fresh green salad for dinner, which didn't disappoint. The chap seemed horrified when I gave him money to cover petrol costs as well as the food. I was equally horrified that he wasn't accepting the money given how much he had gone out of his way to help me not to mention the spiralling cost of petrol. He reluctantly accepted. I hadn't meant to insult him at all. He re-appeared a few moments later with a punnet crammed with grapes and the sweetest local yellow plums as a gift. This clearly meant a lot to him and his wife, who had joined him, and, being a fruit fanatic, I was very happy to accept his lovely gift. They really were such kind-hearted people. I was very touched.

Fully replete with all that delicious food, I felt ready to continue my journey towards the Vosges Mountains tomorrow.

The only downside to today was yet another evil fly bite, this time on my right ankle. I took a photo of how swollen my ankle had become. With its sludgy brown colour and bloated, deformed appearance, it looked as if a bone was broken. The only difficulty was bending the ankle so it was unlikely to be a problem whilst cycling. At least my wonder-cream was earning its keep! Both my arm and calf had recovered from previous bites. I always seemed to get a new bite just as the last one had subsided. The curse of being a tasty snack to these blighters!

Chapter 31 – Monday 13th August 2012: Cycling from Joncherey to Masevaux

Today's first priority was to wish my lovely sister, Janny, a very happy birthday! Her and her partner, Gus, had actually visited and stayed in France over the weekend, just in a completely different region to me. They had been staying in a fairy-tale castle in Normandy. Hmmm, a fairy-tale castle or a flimsy tent… maybe I needed to re-think my accommodation options!

The day had dawned beautifully warm and sunny. How delightful to pack the tent away fully dry. It seemed a bit of a slow start having to go out of my way a few miles to visit the supermarket in Delle first thing. I stocked up with as much as possible until my panniers were fit to burst. Walking around a supermarket with all that tempting and delicious food was akin to a stroll in heaven. I was positively drooling! However, I did have to be sensible about what I could realistically carry. Best of all, I was thrilled to be able to buy several maps, which would see me through at least the next two weeks. That was a great comfort and I could now start to plan properly.

Emerging from the air-conditioned supermarket into the heat of the morning was quite a startling contrast. I knew it had been a warmer morning than usual but it was already feeling really hot and it wasn't even 10am. I would miss this sun and heat as I headed further north so I made the most of this luxurious feeling.

The route today was so pleasant and replicated a gentle roller coaster amongst the fertile agricultural lands that bordered the peaceful road. As I truly left the mountains of the Jura behind, I was surprised to see the outline of the Vosges in the distance. Surely the Vosges couldn't be so close to the Jura? I didn't think I would reach the Vosges until tomorrow and planned to enjoy the much flatter cycling as much as possible before bagging my next cols.

The sun was shining, the birds were singing, the tractors were humming away in the distance. As the Vosges became ever nearer, clouds started to build up in the sky. Everything inside me was screaming "head South, head South!" where it would stay so much warmer. I didn't want to face the worse weather of the North, I was used to the sun and the heat now and I didn't want it to end. I could have cold and rain as often as I wanted in Yorkshire! At least the temperatures didn't feel to be dropping yet, in fact it was becoming increasingly humid and sticky.

This couldn't be right, the Vosges Mountains were looming closer and closer until I found myself cycling right into their foothills. I couldn't believe I only left the Jura yesterday and was now already in the Vosges. They looked further apart on my map and I hadn't exactly been cycling mega distances.

Well, this was a lovely and unexpected treat, the Vosges were spectacular! Their tree-clad peaks were much softer and more round than the Jura. This gave them their name of Ballons des Vosges (like balloon in English). Everywhere, again, was so green and verdant. Fluffy white clouds competed for space in the deep blue sky. Rumbles of thunder could be heard in the distance. Oh dear. Time to find the campsite.

The campsite was very easy to find and was enormous. The site was incredibly well looked after. If I hadn't recently had a rest day, I knew I would be very happy to spend a couple of days here and spend more time exploring the Vosges regional nature reserve.

I chirpily checked in, by now feeling fluent in French at this process. As the lady on reception looked at my passport, she realised I was from the UK and started speaking with a strong Scottish accent! We'd both been speaking in French not realising that we were both from the UK. She had actually lived in Cheltenham for much of her adult life having moved down from Scotland. She and her husband had retired here and looked after this site during the Summer season. What a beautiful place to relocate to and what a fabulous job they did with the site. She advised that a storm was indeed imminent and rain was forecast tomorrow. Boo! Right, time to get the tent up.

The pitches were the flattest I had seen with perfect, manicured grass. The site was extremely well organised and signposted not to mention superbly looked after. The shower blocks were absolutely spotless. There were great facilities. And yet this only achieved 3-star status, the reason being there was no pool. This felt an advantage as the age profile of holidaymakers would otherwise have been much younger and undoubtedly noisier. This place felt more sophisticated as a result. And all this for well under 10 euros.

The storm still seemed to be holding off after I'd got the tent up and showered, so I braved a walk into the nearby town of Masevaux. The first thing I saw around the corner from the campsite was an enormous Super-U supermarket. Typical! I'd carried so much food around all day and hadn't needed to. However, you never know when you'll find a shop or supermarket, especially one that is open, so my number one rule had become buy as much as you can when you can.

Mondays are as dead in France as Sundays, sometimes more so. Almost nothing was open in this entire town. There were some beautiful historic buildings and very pretty flower-filled squares. My swollen insect bitten ankle was starting to give me some grief from walking so I decided to head back. Still the storm seemed to be holding off, just rumbling away in the distance with the odd flash of lightening.

I relaxed over possibly my cheapest and nicest glass of dry white wine of the trip at 1 euro 30. It was so refreshing and delicious but I stuck to my one glass, despite the temptation to indulge in more. I was taking Tramadol painkillers every morning for my arthritic neck. More than one small glass of wine and I would be unconscious!

I couldn't have enjoyed my dinner more. My pan was full to bursting with fresh red and green peppers, courgette, red onion and carrots in a stir-fry sauce whilst the couscous swelled into fluffy fabulousness in my bowl. It was a good job I adored stir-fries, they are my staple diet at home, and they are super-easy to manage on a campstove. Yoghurt and compote with fresh fruit followed, of course, and finally tea and biscuits. I had a very happy belly at the end of this little lot!

It had been another fairly flat, easy and low mileage day of 31 miles. I therefore decided I was now qualified to write "The Slackers Guide to Cycle Touring". I acknowledged I was feeling uncertain about making up routes as I went along and had opted for two shorter days to get me to the top of my current map. This was already building my confidence, which was great. I now felt I needed to incorporate more cycling into my days, particularly if I wanted to cycle all the way to Calais in time to catch the Bike Bus at the end of August.

Perusing my new maps, I set about planning my next day's ride with this in mind. I knew I definitely wanted to cycle up the Grand Ballons d'Alsace. I'd seen photos of this strikingly beautiful area on the internet one lunchtime back in the UK when contemplating where I might cycle. I had no intentions of missing this. It looked like the climb would take much of the day as the ascent commenced immediately from Masevaux.

I was astonished that my new maps did not indicate campsites. The French are compulsive campers so this was very unexpected. Perhaps there were too many campsites to note on the maps. Fortunately, I could consult my trusty Blackberry to check whether campsites existed in the places I was planning to cycle to. There appeared to be numerous campsite choices at the end of tomorrow's ride.

The storm that had rumbled and threatened for the last few hours finally decided to head in another direction, leaving me to enjoy a peaceful night camping under clear skies and twinkling stars.

Chapter 32 – Tuesday 14th August 2012: Cycling from Masevaux to Ramonchamp

I love how well I sleep when camping. A night of true deep sleep is such a rarity and a luxury. I know I'm not alone when I say I don't usually sleep so well at home, frequently waking in the early hours of the morning with a busy head and not getting back to sleep. These touring days of fresh air, exercise, good food and enjoyment were helping me get this glorious, high quality sleep at night many people dream of (my daily intake of Tramadol painkillers probably helped too; they'd take down someone the size of Arnold Schwarzenegger).

I wanted to do a few bits in Masevaux before setting off for the day. What a difference being a Tuesday made! Yesterday, Masevaux was a ghost town; today it was a hive of activity with lively chatter, pavement cafes and street stalls. I was able to change my remaining Swiss Franc notes to euros at one of the banks. I popped into the post office to send my Swiss map and French Alps guidebook back to the UK. I was sure I could feel the drop in weight in my panniers. I bought some provisions from Super-U and, not forgetting, my daily pain au chocolat and baguette from a local boulangerie.

An hour later than usual, I was ready for off, feeling virtuous with what I'd already achieved. I was quite sad to leave this lovely town and campsite. It was another town that had earned a special place in my heart.

The first few miles of today's route were straightforward and pleasant on a wide cycle path which gradually wound its way upwards. It would probably have been just as easy to make my way up the main road, it was almost devoid of traffic. However, this cycle path was here and it was very nice to pedal along it. It was fully segregated from the road, sometimes with houses in between. Signs detailed all the facilities available as the path approached each village including cafes and bike shops as well as general stores. I mentioned before France is good with signs! These were so helpful.

I stopped at a nice looking hotel in Sewen as the path drew to an end. I sat on their sunny terrace enjoying a pot of tea. Usually tea came in a small cup (and bizarrely a large jug of milk that would fill the cup several times over) so to have a whole pot of tea was a rare and wonderful treat. I also ate my pain au chocolat here. This is something I still struggle to get my head around in France. It is normal practise to buy pastries from a boulangerie and then eat them whilst having a drink in a café. I still always check that it is OK to do this and I am inevitably met with a surprised "bien sur" (of course).

The "climb proper" started now with steeper but reasonable gradients on the road. The forecast was for rain, however it was currently sunny not to mention very sticky and humid. This made climbing hot and hard work and a very sweat-drenched affair. The road was blissfully quiet. I made good progress, steadily chugging away, happy in my thoughts, admiring the remarkable views as I wound my way ever upwards in the Vosges Mountains.

I received another "chapeau" today from a female cyclist who pedalled alongside me to chat for a while. Hurray! This was amongst plenty of other "bravo", "bon courage" and "bonne chance" messages of support as other cyclists powered their way past me. These guys were pushing so hard, perhaps trying to improve on their personal bests. Their faces were pink with effort. I needed to keep energy in my legs simply to get up the mountain carrying this little lot so attempted to keep a steady pace and something in reserve if I needed it.

As I reached the top of the col, I broke into a huge grin. It had taken 13 kilometres of pedalling continuously uphill to get here. The Col du Ballon was 1,247 metres high (4,091 feet). The scenery was fabulous and worth every pedal stroke. Moreover, I was actually looking at the view that I'd seen on the internet earlier in the year. That very photo had provided inspiration on how to structure my tour post-Switzerland. I was now living that dream. This was another very special moment of the tour.

The descent was the stuff cycling dreams are made of – lots of straight, smooth sections with none of the hairpin bends too tight or technical. It was the sort of descent that made me feel as free as a bird and wanting to whoop with delight. I waved at all the cyclists toiling upwards, with particular shouts of support for the only other fully laden cycle-tourer I had seen so far. I waved like a crazy woman and he, despite his heavy camping load, was waving madly back with a massive grin at this show of support and solidarity.

At the bottom of the descent, I was flung straight onto a very busy and noisy main road. This wasn't ideal, however I only had a handful of miles to cycle to Le Thillot, my destination for the day. At least I noted that Le Thillot was a large town with plenty of shopping facilities as I cycled through, following the signs to the campsite.

2-3 miles later, I realised I must have completely missed the sign to the big family campsite on the outskirts of Le Thillot. How bizarre. Never mind, I had just picked up signs for another campsite a couple of hundred yards away in Ramonchamp. The campsite in Le Thillot would have been full of families with lots of noise, life and laughter. The campsite at Ramonchamp was more suited to me as a solo cycle tourist – it was very small and peaceful with only the most basic of facilities. This was perfect for me.

I pitched up under a tree on the flat, grassy field and alongside a gurgling river. A small but perfectly formed shower block stood in the middle of the field with everything I needed – a hot shower, spotlessly clean facilities and, very unusually for France, toilet paper!

I nearly fell over when the owner told me the price was a mere 4 euros 12. I could do with more of these campsites, please!

My cycling mileage was quite low at 30 miles again however at least I'd climbed a mountain today, so the distance was understandable and I felt that I'd actually cycled throughout the day rather than coasted.

My legs were very tired and I was glad I didn't have to walk far to the nearest bar for my glass of chilled white. It was still so humid late in the afternoon with temperatures approaching the 30s. That was probably why I felt more debilitated than usual. There was no sun, just oppressive heavy cloud. Thankfully, it hadn't rained as forecast.

After relaxing over my drink, I located the "voie verte", the green-way or cycle path, which would be the start of tomorrow's ride. It looked relatively easy for the first few miles, simply cycling across this basin, surrounded by the verdant Vosges Mountains.

I fell asleep for 45 minutes when I got back to the tent before cooking dinner, most unlike me. I was feeling just slightly under the weather, quite achy with a bit of a temperature. I was craving a French omelette, chips and salad but another stir-fry with couscous and a sweet and sour sauce was on the menu to use up all of my veggies. I was confident this fresh, vitamin packed dinner and another good night's sleep in this peaceful place would do the trick and get me fully back on my feet.

Chapter 33 – Wednesday 15th August 2012; Cycling from Ramonchamp to Vittel

I felt back on top form this morning and fully restored after a solid night's sleep and eating my favourite meal of the day, breakfast. I was relieved my milk had survived overnight without going off in the humidity. Conditions were still very sticky as I packed everything up and loaded the bike. I was relieved to know I would be pedalling in the midst of vast, peaceful fields on the voie verte rather than the busy main road for the first few miles today.

I had planned my route to head towards Vittel. I had already cycled through the busy town of Evian along the shores of Lac Leman, it would be nice to continue the theme and include another famous mineral water town on this tour.

Just as I was leaving, my closest camping neighbours popped over to say hello and ask where I was touring. They were delighted when they discovered I was English, they proudly told me their dogs were English, too. Initially confused, I realised what they meant when I saw their adorable little dogs were Yorkshire Terriers. Amused, I told them I was actually from Yorkshire, the county their dogs were named after. They were ecstatic! They bade me farewell and wished me all the very best for the rest of my trip. I thoroughly enjoyed such friendly encounters from complete strangers, they were the icing on the cake as far as my tour was concerned. I was also pleased I had sufficient French to manage such conversations.

I cycled along in my own happy little world, pedalling on the voie verte, gazing up at the tree-clad mountains surrounding the deep basin I was cycling through. I had a tailwind, making progress very satisfying.

Once back on the roads, they were again blissfully quiet. This is one of the reasons I truly love cycling in France. It is so very different from our traffic-clogged nation.

I chose routes as I went along, just making sure I was heading in the general direction of Vittel. It was very hot and humid and the lack of water fountains was making this very dry and thirsty work. I'm sure many cyclists reading this will know exactly what it is like to drink disgusting warm water from plastic bidons on your bike. It does not quench your thirst and can make you feel quite nauseous.

About 25 miles into the day whilst cycling along, minding my own business, a car came past me and slowed right down. The occupants were waving like crazy. I was perplexed; I didn't know anyone in France. I looked on in confusion until I saw the heads of two little Yorkshire Terriers pop up over the back seat. It was my neighbours from this morning! Delighted, I waved back in an equally crazy manner. They waved lots more once they realised I'd recognised them before driving off.

All that waving, smiling and excitement wore me out! I stopped for refreshments in Remiremont. I found a nice boulangerie selling homemade Gruyere quiche. I couldn't resist buying one for lunch along with my usual baguette. As I continued to stroll around, I became baffled. So many shops in this large town seemed to be closed. What did the French now have against Wednesdays? I later discovered that today was yet another French Bank Holiday. Honestly, when do the French work?! I envy their life-work balance.

I really struggled to cycle out of the town. I tried pretty much every route out of Remiremont but couldn't find the next village I was aiming for. There were major roadworks throughout the town with diversions in place, which certainly didn't help. Diversions to where? When in doubt, I generally head for roundabouts as they are usually very well sign posted. All the big roundabouts in the town had been taken over by roadworks though. I went backwards and forwards for nearly an hour before heading down a major road in frustration and then heading back again when I picked up the right sign. I nearly went back to the café I'd just been to for another cuppa! As the temperature was now well into the 30s, this lengthy messing around and detour had been dusty, hot and thirsty work.

To add to my annoyance, I passed a large bike shop. I'd been wanting to get my bike tyres blown up for several days. Of course, the shop was shut with today being a Bank Holiday.

Once back on the right track and peaceful roads, I relaxed back into the rhythm of pedalling along whilst enjoying the scenery. The terrain rolled up and down with nothing too steep or long.

My biggest climb of the day was up Col du Poirier, however at just over 450 metres, this was not exactly the Alpine standard of previous weeks.

The sun came out and the temperature felt to instantly double. I was getting desperate for water. I'd need to find a café or shop, or even someone in their garden, to obtain fresh supplies. Should I be concerned that I was considering drinking from garden hoses? My mouth was bone dry.

As I cycled into the small town of Xertigny, I spotted a shady bench underneath the remarkably grand and imposing town hall. That would make a good picnic spot. I needed to get my hot helmet-head out of the sun. I was surprisingly hungry to say it was so hot. My cheese was starting to sweat rather alarmingly and was becoming rubbery in the heat. The fresh tomato in my sandwich was refreshingly juicy. Fortunately, the quiche had survived mostly intact and was also absolutely delicious.

I'd seen a lady looking at me as I wolfed down my feast. She'd disappeared back into the cool of the nearby small tourist office. I hoped she would allow me to fill up my water bottles from the tap in the tourist office.

Not only did she let me fill my water bottles with cool, fresh water, she was so pleased to have someone to talk to that I was there for nearly another hour! She knew a little English from the short time she had spent in "twee" Kent, so between her English, my French and "Google Translate" on her computer, we managed quite a conversation! She explained that the weather was unusually hot (no kidding). I think she said it was due to winds from the Sahara. This north-eastern region of France was currently hotter than the Mediterranean and was set to get hotter every day this week. And I'd been worried about heading to the cooler, cloudier, wetter north! This inevitably meant more storms later in the week though. When I eventually departed, she waved me off like a long lost friend.

My much-appreciated tailwind became a much stronger and persistent headwind as I continued to cycle in the direction of Vittel. With no real mountains to climb today, I was eating up the miles and wondering if I might even make it to Vittel today.

I hadn't thought this was possible looking at the map yesterday. This thought spurred me on and I pushed on into the wind with gusto.

The road started to climb gently and continued to do so for several miles. My goodness, this was becoming exhausting work. The incessant incline, the sticky heat, the interminable headwind, the dragging weight of my panniers, my slightly deflated tyres creating more drag on the road. I spotted not too far ahead something else the French do incredibly well: picnic spots under shady trees. Perfect!

I continued to fight against the wind and slowly but surely pedalled my way towards the picnic spot at the top of this long climb. It was worth the effort. I was rewarded with terrific views across the countryside. The trees sheltered me more from the increasing strength of the wind as well as the sun. I took some time to eat, drink and rest. I knew it was mostly downhill all the way into Vittel now. This thought perked me up.

I swept downhill into Vittel to be greeted by yet another ghost town. I'd promised myself that omelette, chips and salad I'd been dreaming about tonight to celebrate cycling 64 miles, but that clearly wasn't going to happen. Vittel was much smaller than Evian albeit with some pretty buildings. I circuited the town on my bike to see if any shops were open. Nope. However, there was an ice-cream vendor. I dreamt of climbing into the ice-cream freezers to cool down. I managed to restrain myself and ordered my favourite combo of a chocolate and vanilla ice-cream with the added bonus of a chocolate flake. That wouldn't last long in this heat!

I literally nose-dived into the ice-cream. It cooled my lips and mouth down instantly. I devoured it at great speed needing its cooling benefits immediately. I coughed and spluttered as my asthma protested. I didn't care, this was fabulous and a well-earned treat.

Feeling vaguely human again, I needed to locate the campsite. I found some signs and started heading up the hill. Why are campsites always up hills? As I reached the top of this hill, I was directed up another hill and then another. Just as my levels of frustration were starting to take over, the campsite thankfully came into view. I was so incredibly hot and thirsty again. I was personally melting faster than any ice-cream.

The guy looking after the campsite practised his English as I spoke in French to book in. This campsite had standard pitches segregated by high hedges that were mostly occupied by motorhomes and caravans. The pitches were quite rocky and stony rather than nice and grassy. Never mind, I was able to drive most of my tent pegs into the ground. I had found a lovely pitch tucked away in a corner that was close to fresh water taps and not far from the scrupulously clean shower block.

I'm all for a powerful shower, however these showers had a ferocious jet of water that pretty much blasted you out of the building. One little girl was crying, the water hurt her so much. It was indeed quite a challenge trying to shower. Great care was needed when rinsing the shampoo out of my hair not to let the water jet hammer my head into my shoulders. The water was nice and hot though. I know many people like cold showers in such heat but I still like them hot. I feel much cleaner and more relaxed afterwards.

The town was too far away to walk so I set about making dinner from my latest emergency supplies. I had some dried mushroom risotto that simply needed water adding to it and heating. The packet was for four people and I heated the majority of it. There was no need to be shy. I was delighted to see a fresh carrot, courgette and tomato had more or less survived the day, so they were added to the dish. The risotto had a wonderful depth of flavour and I thoroughly enjoyed every delicious mouthful.

Dark clouds were gathering overhead as I drank my big mug of tea. I'd seen at the tourist office this morning that storms had been forecast later in the week so I wasn't unduly concerned. It would still probably be best to get the pots and pans washed up straight away in case it did start raining though. I took my phone to recharge at the same time and my waterproof jacket, just in case.

A vicious thunderstorm broke out as I reached the shower block. It was still raging 40 minutes later, my washing up long done and my phone nicely recharged. I stood waiting for a suitable moment to make a run for it back to the tent. Catching sight of myself in one of the few mirrors, I realised how incredibly tanned I'd become. I hadn't had a tan in years! That kept my spirits up!

I needed to make a dash back to the tent. Although it wasn't far, I was drenched in seconds. Thank goodness I'd brought my waterproof with me. I tried to get into the tent without soaking everything inside. Even though it wasn't late, I needed to put the tent light on to write my diary and blog, plan tomorrow's route and read my Kindle. By 9pm, the thunder and lightening had abated but the rain continued battering the tent mercilessly. I hated my bike being out and exposed in these conditions.

The best thing I could do was hunker down and hope the weather would vastly improve by tomorrow. I would certainly be grateful for less sticky conditions.

Chapter 34 – Thursday 16th August 2012: Cycling from Vittel to Thonnance les Moulins

I had a fairly disturbed sleep last night as the torrential rain continued unabated. Thankfully, the morning dawned dry and bright although I had to pack my tent away absolutely saturated. I dried off my trusty workhorse of a bike as best I could, paying particular attention to the chain and ensuring it was sufficiently oiled.

I ate my breakfast in the serene park in the centre of Vittel once the shops were back open and I was able to buy some milk. I also stocked up as much as I could from the local Spar as, according to my map, places of civilisation looked few and far between on today's ride.

The storm had helped clear the air a little although the temperatures remained in the mid to late 20s as the day progressed.

Today's 50 miles of cycling was a cyclist's dream pedalling along exceptionally quiet roads that gently rolled with pleasant views of the surrounding countryside. The price to pay for this piece of heaven was no shops, no cafes, no bars, no water, no facilities. You can't have everything! None of the limited number of small hamlets I passed through had any shops. I wondered how they survived. I guess they commute to larger towns and buy provisions when they are there.

I did pass a large Super-U supermarket early in the afternoon. There had been signs for this supermarket for the last few miles, they seemed to sponsor most of the surrounding villages including the local school. However, it was shut!! Apparently many supermarkets in rural France close between 12pm – 2pm for lunch! It was in between this time. I decided not to wait. I was so astounded. It is so very different from the 24/7 culture in the UK. Which country has it right?

I cycled from the Vosges region into the Champagne-Ardennes region today. It felt like another notable achievement and more good progress in the right direction towards Calais. I was hoping to make it into the main Champagne region by the weekend and spend some time there. An exciting thought!

In keeping with the lack of facilities in this region, I was also lacking any campsites and, come to mention it, any guesthouses. I had started to pick up signs for a campsite in Thonnance and a quick check on my Blackberry confirmed it did indeed still exist. Excellent, it was worth cycling further than I had planned to today.

The campsite was more of a holiday park, once again dominated by motorhomes and caravans. Having paid anywhere between 4 euros to 10 euros since being in this region of France, I nearly fell over when they asked for 25 euros. I stammered that I had a small tent and would not be using the swimming pool, tennis courts and every other facility they had on their site, I simply needed a place to pitch for the evening. They were having none of it and they knew they had me cornered – I was in the middle of precisely nowhere with no hope of another campsite for miles. It was also late afternoon and I was tired.

Very reluctantly I accepted. The pitches were of very poor quality again, all rocky, hard and stony. I was not impressed for the price. I erected my tent in the far corner of my allocated pitch, which was the grassiest bit I could find and the only spot where I had a hope of the pegs going in. At least it was warm and sunny allowing the tent to dry out after last night's storm.

Despite the price of this campsite, it was undeniably in the most stunning setting (but then so were many of my much cheaper campsites!).

This site did have a small shop, a pizzeria and a restaurant. Ooo, maybe I could get my omelette, chips and salad tonight! I was able to buy some milk for tomorrow's breakfast. I also bought a large can of ratatouille as my next emergency back up. It was heavy to carry but the only option available and definitely better than nothing. I was always happier when I had some emergency supplies.

The site redeemed itself with a large glass of white wine for 1 euro 50 during their happy hour. They didn't have omelette on the menu however they did have a veggie option of a cheese quiche, chips and salad. That along with lots of bread would be good carbo-loading. I even treated myself to a dessert of their red berry cheesecake. Yum! I had a little chuckle to myself that I needed to wear my fluffy fleece as the evening temperatures dipped whilst everyone else remained wearing vest tops and shorts. How do they do it? You can understand why I'm better suited to a hot, sunny climate!

A live band started to play just as I was finishing dinner. The music was actually very good and I found myself bopping along in my tent for a while afterwards. I felt sorry for those starting to dine though, they couldn't possibly have a conversation with such loud music and singing. Despite the ground reverberating with the noise well into the night, I did manage to sleep through.

Chapter 35 – Friday 17th August 2012: Cycling from Thonnance les Moulins to Vitry le Francois

It was a surprisingly chilly start to the day although I was pleased as this meant the milk had stayed deliciously cool overnight making for a very refreshing breakfast. I was up and away long before most people on the site had even stirred. It was always special having the morning to myself.

I wasn't expecting to climb for my first 2 miles of the day but at least this helped warm me up. The area was heavily forested and the sun hadn't yet broken through. I enjoyed some sweeping descents and then the countryside rolled like a rollercoaster making for another very pleasant day of cycling.

I stopped early in the day in a small town called Joinville. Although it had no cafes, they did have a boulangerie where I could stock up for lunch. I had wanted a café to celebrate me hitting the 1,000 mile mark on this trip. My celebrations would have to wait until I could find a place with a café. Based on recent experience, it might be a few days wait!

As it happened, I didn't have to wait too long. The temperatures were already soaring well into the 30s as the morning progressed. I cycled into the small town of Wassy which did have a café, albeit indoors. This indoor café in Wassy and the indoor swimming pool at the campsite in Thonnance that I left this morning suggested this area was not used to such heat and sunshine. Well, I wanted to celebrate and this might be the only café I came across all day.

Stepping inside was a bit like stepping inside a cowboy salon whereby everybody and everything stops to stare at The Stranger. Gulp! I quietly ordered my tea and retreated to the far corner, pretending to bury myself in the local newspaper. The other customers were openly looking at me and pointing. It was quite strange and slightly unnerving. Normally, people would approach me or they'd leave me alone. This was new territory.

I silently congratulated myself on reaching 1,000 miles on the tour and then got up to pay and leave. One of the guys came over to ask me a question. I didn't catch what he said, so explained I was English and that I was on a cycle tour. More questions suddenly followed with people leaning in, interested in what I had to say. Before long, everyone had joined in, asking me questions, declaring me very brave for doing this solo and patting me on the back for my achievements so far. By the time I left, the whole café wished me well on the rest of my journey and waved me off. Wow, what a turnaround of events in the small locality of Wassy!

More support followed as I cycled through another small hamlet later in the day. A little old lady was hobbling out of her front door, barely able to move. I smiled and bade her bonjour. Her face creased into a wide smile and she raised her fist in the air with a triumphant "bravo!". This wonderful show of support kept me going the rest of the day. I felt invincible with that little old lady's enthusiasm for what I was doing.

For lunch, I deviated off route to enjoy one of the beaches alongside the impressive and vast Lac du Der. I found some picnic tables under some shady trees and did my best to enjoy a picnic of sweaty, rubbery cheese with extra tomatoes for juice and moisture. My picnic table overlooked part of the lake with lots of people enjoying the cool waters as the temperatures soared ever higher. The place had a real upbeat holiday feel.

I was fortunate to have some excellent sun-cream. Normally, I have very pale skin but thankfully my skin had become accustomed to the hot sunny conditions over the weeks and the sun-cream had protected it brilliantly. Today, it felt the sun-cream was being washed off in rivers of sweat but the protection seemed to be holding well.

The temperature continued to climb throughout the afternoon. The sweat poured. All thoughts of tired legs, a tight neck and shoulders and saddle soreness were replaced by an indescribable and overwhelming thirst and the driest mouth I think I have ever experienced. There didn't seem to be anywhere to get any water. I was still looking for hosepipes in gardens to drink from! All the hamlets and villages I passed through seemed deserted. Where was everyone?

I arrived into Vitry le Francois, beyond delighted and relieved to see a café. I promptly plonked myself down and ordered a chilled glass of apricot juice followed by a pot of tea and the very kind lady serving me filled my water bottles with ice-cold water which were also immediately consumed.

At this stage, I planned to continue further into the Champagne region. Once I had sat down and rested, I knew it would be hard to get going again, particularly in this heat. It was already mid-afternoon. I checked on the Blackberry and there was apparently a campsite in this town. My next mission was to find it.

I pulled myself up and, just as I set off, saw the first sign for the campsite. It was fate! I followed the signs for the campsite through this pleasingly large town, which had a supermarket, plenty of (open!) shops and lots of other cafes and restaurants. Thank goodness, facilities at last!

The campsite was almost empty, I think there were two other families there in this considerable space. That was no problem for me. The price of 4 euros 70 was also a very welcome relief after my expensive night in Thonnance yesterday. I had everything I needed here including a real grassy pitch!

I got the tent up and went for a shower. The shampoo was so hot, it nearly burnt my head. The tent had dried to a crisp by the time I returned. Just as I walked around the tent to tend to the bike, there was a large CRACK! My tent completely collapsed with everything in it. Oh my goodness! The key tent pole at the front had completely broken and splintered.

After the initial few seconds of shock, I pulled myself together, remembering there was something in my tent bag to help in the unlikely event of a tent pole breaking. Phew! The tent bag was reasonably easy to locate under the material of the collapsed front porch. The saviour was a simple "sleeve" to slip over the broken pole, enabling the pole to perform its normal duty.

This would have been fine had the broken pole not been so badly splintered. I tried standing on the broken metal to reduce it down in order to slip the sleeve on. It wasn't working. I decided to get help from the campsite reception. I was sure they would have come across this before. The lady came out with me to examine the tent and I did my best to explain in French. Exclaiming "ooo la la", she went in search of her husband who in turn went to retrieve his pliers. Fortunately, he had very strong hands and was – just – able to reduce the splintered metal sufficiently to get the sleeve on. What a relief.

I un-pegged the tent and re-pitched it with its temporary pole. It seemed to go up OK. I had concerns about putting the tent up and down on a daily basis for the rest of the trip – would this broken pole hold? The sleeve seemed completely stuck and welded on. If not, I reasoned I could jump on a train to the nearest town and buy a replacement tent if the worst came to the worst. That wasn't too awful a scenario.

I had anticipated something going wrong with the bike during the trip but hadn't contemplated anything going wrong with the tent. I had only bought it last year. I'd done extensive research before buying it and knew from forums in what high regard this product was held, particularly in adverse weather conditions. And yet mine had collapsed in perfect conditions, if admittedly very hot. Never mind, it was all now sorted and I had a town with exciting shops and facilities to explore!

First things first, a glass of wine to calm my jangled nerves! I found some tables in the much-needed shade and relaxed as I sipped my refreshing drink, caught up on my diary writing and watched the world go by. Vitry was a large town and I was sat overlooking the impressive and imposing archway to the town.

After perusing a few menus of nearby restaurants, my elusive omelette dinner remained so. After last night's quiche, bread and chips, I was in need of lots of fresh vegetables so another stir-fry made on my trusty Trangia beckoned. I was able to purchase several pouches of different stir-fry sauces from the local supermarket as well as lots of lovely fresh vegetables. The interior of the supermarket was also clearly the coolest place in town, fabulously air-conditioned against the baking heat outside.

My main concern with cooking now was turning back to my dwindling gas supplies. I needed to find another Decathlon. Looking up the nearest store on my Blackberry, I located one in Chalons-en-Champagne, a town I would soon be passing through.

My dinner was as tasty as always. Eating is one of life's greatest pleasures and I always enjoyed my healthy, colourful, nutritious stir-fries. My portion sizes were huge but I felt this was justified with the amount of cycling I was doing and the fact that I was mainly eating vegetables. The yoghurt for dessert had just about survived the temperatures since returning from the supermarket. I feared my milk wouldn't survive overnight. I could only try and found the most shaded spot under the trees next to my tent to keep it as cool as possible.

Looking at the map for the next few days, I decided to stay here another night and enjoy a rest day tomorrow. The forecast showed the temperatures reaching 40 degrees tomorrow. I could manage physically cycling in such heat, the biggest issue was the lack of cool drinking water or anywhere to buy liquid en route. I also decided the main Champagne region I had originally planned to cycle to tomorrow would be very busy on a Saturday and camping may be hard to come across. It would be a safer bet on Sunday night. Unless the campsite at Vitry were expecting a huge influx tomorrow, there was certainly no issue with space here and I was very happy to be so close to a town. It would be nice to get the laundry done, too. I hoped there would be a bike shop in the town where I could get my tyres properly pumped up.

Decision made, I attempted to settle down for as decent a night's sleep as I could manage in my hot and sticky state. Concerns about the tent collapsing on me in the middle of the night were at the forefront of my mind. What will be, will be. I'd deal with it if it happened. Right now, I simply needed to get some sleep.

Chapter 36 – Saturday 18th August 2012: Rest Day in Vitry le Francois

I fortunately did manage to get some sleep last night, particularly as the temperatures cooled in the early hours of the morning. There had been some fireworks overnight, I'm not sure what for. Perhaps that is how the French celebrate the end of the week in this neck of the woods!

Both my tent and the milk had survived overnight. I was therefore able to enjoy a very relaxing breakfast overlooking the mature gardens of the empty campsite first thing in the morning.

There were no washing machines here so I did the laundry in the big clothes washing sinks with masses of sweet smelling shampoo. I wondered wryly why I was bothering – these clothes would be soaked in sweat and salt within minutes of putting them back on. It was always worth clean, fresh smelling clothes though. There were some handy clothes lines for me to hang everything out on before venturing into town.

I'd packed up a few more maps and diaries from my earlier days to send back home. I found a bookshop selling maps and was able to buy the final map I needed to get me to Calais.

I bought a pain aux raisins from the boulangerie, a change from my usual pain au chocolat, to enjoy with a cup of tea at a nearby café. As always, I checked again that it was OK to consume food at the café that I had bought from elsewhere and was met with the usual surprised "bien sur". I explained this was not possible in the UK to which the shocked reply was "how severe".

I surprised my Mum with a phone call. She had still been fast asleep in bed! I updated her on my trip, she updated me with all the work she was having done on the house. It was very lovely to hear her voice and have a taste of home. The French heat wave had clearly not made its way to UK shores with rain still prominent in many parts of the country.

The air-conditioned supermarket was my next port of call, I needed to cool down! I bought some fresh lettuce, tomatoes and avocadoes to accompany the home-made quiche and baguette I already had bought for lunch. Back at the campsite, there were some picnic tables under a copse of trees where I was able to eat in the shade. It was far too hot to sit anywhere near the tent in direct sunlight. The temperature was approaching 40 degrees. Rivers of sweat ran off me as I chopped up the salad for lunch.

I had a short snooze in the afternoon before heading back into town. I wandered around the supermarket again simply to cool my temperature down before heading to a nearby café for some ice-cream. At the café, they were automatically serving everyone with large jugs of ice-cold water for free. The ice melted within minutes. The ice-cream needed to be demolished equally quickly before it became melted goo. I also had a pot of tea, which I find quite refreshing in the heat. The poor waiters were really struggling in the extreme temperatures but remained fully professional.

I went back to the supermarket for a final cool down and to buy some filled tortellini pasta to accompany the remaining salad and bread for dinner. After spending a few hours in the tent, the lettuce had pretty much boiled in the bag and the tomato wasn't in a much better condition. This had quite possibly been the hottest day I'd ever experienced whilst camping. It was all part of the fun!

I was really keen to get going on the bike again, despite the heat. I thought an earlier start would be the best approach and to pitch up at the next campsite by mid-afternoon. The real heat of the day was felt late afternoon. That heat would be useful to dry my cycling clothes each night! I guessed finding fresh water would be an issue, I'd just have to drink what I could when I could.

Looking at the maps, I was daring to believe that, all being well, I could cycle all the way to Calais now without having to catch a train to make it in time for the Bike Bus home. I was taking everything a day at a time, never looking too far forward and always enjoying the present moment as much as possible. Whether this was shivering in snow covered mountains or melting in the current heatwave, all my experiences were amazing and making this tour what it was. Yes, even the broken tent pole incident! I didn't yet know if I could dismantle the tent and re-erect it again. I suppose I would find out tomorrow.

Chapter 37 – Sunday 19th August 2012: Cycling from Vitry le Francois to Fismes

I slept like an absolute log last night, despite the heat. I awoke with a very stiff and painful neck, which is never fun. I thought arthritis was usually worst in cold, damp conditions not boiling hot weather. I worked to get it moving again and downed my trusty painkillers earlier than usual.

After a lovely breakfast, I was packed up and off by 8am. I was so relieved when I dismantled the tent with no issue. It packed away perfectly, too, I thought the broken pole with the sleeve on would really stick out and I'd already planned how to cope with this on the bike. Fortunately, it wasn't a problem.

The countryside rolled beautifully and I planned to have a cuppa in Chalons-en-Champagne as well as locate the Decathlon there to buy some more gas canisters. Agh, it was Sunday – everything was shut! Sigh, I would need to find another store later on. My remaining gas canister would last a bit longer, I just wasn't sure how long. If only they came with a warning when they were about to run out!

I realised how huge Chalons-en-Champagne was and, after taking so long to find my way out of Remiremont the other day, I wasn't risking the same again. Instead, I stopped at the junction where I needed to turn off, ate my pain au chocolat and drank some water before continuing all the way to Epernay.

I'd assumed I would be cycling amongst vineyards given I was in the Champagne region. However, I didn't see any until I literally cycled into Epernay, the heart of the Champagne region itself. In the heat, I thought I was going slightly mad and surely there would be vineyards somewhere.

The approach into Epernay was amazing, cycling along the cobbled streets and past all the 19th century mansions housing the headquarters of prestigious and world famous champagne houses such as Moet and Chandon and Mercier. Unfortunately, I seemed to be holding up lots of traffic so had to keep moving. Typically, there had been literally no traffic until this point.

Upon reaching the main roundabout into the town, I saw a café that was open and dived into it for several gallons of tea. Again, they very kindly re-filled my water bottles with ice-cold water even adding ice-cubes to keep it chilled for as long as possible. Just putting the water bottles to my face and neck helped cool me down a little. Cycling was helping in the heat by creating a breeze.

I couldn't wait to look around Epernay. I cycled into a large square with a pretty water fountain and ate my picnic lunch here. I looked around. Every shop was shut. Even more irritating, I was eating my lunch on a bench right next to another large bike shop, which, of course, was closed. Unbelievable! (Actually, I couldn't believe I was eating cheese in such a melted, congealed state either.) There were a few people milling around but not many. I had planned to stay at the local campsite tonight but I started to reconsider. I wouldn't be able to see very much given everything was closed. It was extremely hot. And I still had plenty of energy left for cycling.

I consulted the map. I'd done 42 miles, there was the threat of a storm in the afternoon but I didn't fancy staying Epernay. Fismes looked the next best destination and I confirmed that it had a campsite. Excellent, I had a new plan.

Cycling through the neat rows of vineyards in the Champagne region felt really special and I smiled the whole way through, trying to keep the bike steady as I looked from side to side to ensure I wasn't missing anything. The road was climbing out of the town and it wasn't long before the sweat started to pour down my face, neck, arms and legs again.

It was starting to cloud over. Although it was helpful to not be cycling in direct searing sun, it felt even stickier under the clouds.

I seemed to be going upwards more than I thought. And then the really steep climbs started. Blimey, this truly wasn't what I needed in these blistering conditions. I stood up on the bike to push down hard on the pedals to get them to turn. The gradient had jumped to Yorkshire Dales proportions and went on for considerably longer. My face must have been purple, it certainly felt it. My throat was parched. My hands were so wet with sweat, they were slipping on the handlebars. A guy came past in a car with English registration plates and 3 bicycles on the roof rack. The driver proclaimed me his hero. Even this didn't pick my spirits up in the usual way. I wondered what I was doing and why on earth I'd made the decision to leave Epernay. I was apparently climbing in the "Montagnes de Reims", which translates as the "mountains of Reims", the nearby city. How had I managed to find the only mountains in the Champagne region?

The agonising climb eventually eased. As I continued to cycle through a number of villages, I heard a sound that was music to my ears. Gushing water. Please, please, please be a freshwater drinking fountain. A sign declaring "NON-POTABLE" was stuck firmly across this water fountain. The cruelty. Crushed, I threw the cool water over myself in an attempt to cool down. I dunked the water bottles in to try to cool the water inside them down as well.

Another village a few miles later and more sounds of gushing water. This elaborate water fountain had water cascading from every direction. Again, the "NON-POTABLE" sign was stuck firmly across. I decided I didn't care. I was absolutely desperate, my throat and mouth as dry as bark. I downed bottleful after bottleful of water and continued to throw it over myself. Once I'd started, I couldn't stop. I wouldn't necessarily recommend doing this but that was my state of mind at the time. I guessed that water had flowed into this fountain for over a century without issue. The risk was worth it to me on that day at that time.

I've never felt so much better after downing so much water. I felt entirely re-hydrated. I knew I would be hot again soon but this had been such sweet and necessary relief on this sizzling hot day.

Fismes was a very pleasant small town with, as usual, absolutely nothing open. The temperature was showing 39 degrees in the late afternoon. I noted a café would be open in the evening in case I wanted to pop back in later. The campsite was a good 1-2 kilometres further away, mostly downhill, which made a welcome change. It was unusually located on an industrial estate and next door to some sports fields. The land was very flat in this area so it did make sense.

There was no-one on reception and, in fact, no-one around at all. This was quite a small site. A notice invited you to pitch up until someone was available. I was happy to oblige and keen to get showered, my clothes washed and hung out to dry. As soon as the tent was pitched, thankfully without issue, the broken pole holding up perfectly, I headed for the shower block. I then saw the doors had keypads on. The doors were locked. I tried some obvious combinations, such as 1234, but to no avail. I went back to the noticeboard to see if there was the key code written on there somewhere. No. To my alarm, I then noticed that reception was now closed until Monday morning 8.30am. What?? How did anyone go to the loo then? It was mid-afternoon on Sunday. This was bizarre. Why were the doors locked and key-coded? There was absolutely no evidence of any crime here, in fact there wasn't really evidence of any people.

It's harder to think straight when tired and in such scorching heat. It's easier to feel irrational and frustrated instead. I calmed myself down and tried to call some of the telephone numbers on the noticeboard that were advised if reception was closed. It wasn't always easy to translate what the board was trying to tell me. Of course, there was no answer anywhere because it was Sunday afternoon and all offices were shut.

Half in desperation and half thinking they could help, I decided to call the local police. Yes, I know, had I completely lost my mind? The local police have a big part to play in these local communities so I genuinely thought they might have the key code for their municipal campsite. I battled through in French as best I could, very much hoping they got the gist. A baffled policeman on the other end of the line asked "Madame, what would you like me to do?". I asked if they had the key code, which was met with a definite no. I asked if they had a telephone number of someone I could call. He asked around the station and, incredibly, to the astonishment of this policeman, someone in the background said yes. They gave me a number, I wish I could have hugged them all!

I called this number, a man answered, we tried some combinations on the keypad and, given nothing was working, he said he'd drive over and would be with me in the next few minutes. True to his word, he arrived. I had a pad and pen at the ready, not trusting myself to remember anything today. The access code to the ladies shower block was a complicated mix of numbers and letters. Amusingly, access to the men's was a simple 1234 code with a letter at the end! I was so deliriously happy. The guy commended me on my French (really?!) and we chatted about my tour before he drove away.

Never have I appreciated a shower and a toilet so much! I have no idea what campers normally do if they turn up after 9am on a Sunday. This can't have been the first time this issue has arisen. You simply can't have people going to the loo in the campsite field! That's even more bizarre than me calling the police in desperation!

Showered and refreshed, I set about making dinner. I had the large can of ratatouille, which I have to say exceeded all expectations, I thought it might be quite dire. I had fresh veg of my own that had survived the day and ate the lot with plenty of fluffy couscous.

I felt the need to go for a stroll and loosen off my legs. I'd cycled 70 miles today, including the ascent of the mountains of Reims (not true mountains but very long, steep hills nonetheless) and dealt with the police. It had been quite a day.

The café I'd spotted earlier was now buzzing with life and activity. I was wooed by the extraordinary array of sorbets, opting for 3 different flavours, which I had with a jug of ice-cold water. It was deliciously cool in the café compared to outside.

As I arrived back at the campsite, a number of motorhomes and caravans had turned up. All were wandering around considering how to get into the shower block. Andi to the rescue!! I became the official campsite hero for knowing the access codes! I should have charged for my knowledge and power! I was offered food and drink, anything I wanted. I laughed, knowing exactly how they were feeling. But mostly, I was looking forward to settling down for the night after a long, hot and adventurous day.

Chapter 38 – Monday 20th August 2012: Cycling from Fismes to Laon

Today was officially my "Grump Day" of the tour. Perhaps it's a Monday thing?

Perhaps most likely it was the thought that exactly one week today, I would be catching the Bike Bus in Calais and making my way home. I was enjoying myself far too much for this tour to be anywhere near over.

In addition, the heat, the continual grind of cycling up so many hills (wasn't it supposed to be flat now?), dealing with creaking, sore and aching body parts and particularly the ongoing difficulty of buying and keeping fresh food were all starting to take their toll. I had expected to experience some lows as well as highs on this trip so these feelings didn't come as a total surprise and I allowed myself to wallow for a while (affectionately known as "hippo-time"). I knew I was enjoying the trip immensely overall and knew I would still rather be here than anywhere else, grump or otherwise. I therefore permitted myself to finish early today although, in hindsight, the spot I chose probably exacerbated The Grump!

To start at the beginning, I needed to wait for the nearby Aldi to open in Fismes at 8am to buy some cold, fresh milk for my cereal in addition to some other bits and pieces for the day. You can only imagine The Grump intensifying if I don't get my favourite meal of the day or if it is delayed! I'd packed everything up as far as possible to ensure a swift departure after eating. I was still being offered food and drink by others on the campsite for my help in enabling them to access the shower block. I was quite enjoying my hero status!

The police turned up whilst I was eating my breakfast as well. Oh no! My phone call yesterday had clearly triggered something and I was feeling really bad, I didn't want to cause any trouble. Considering the number of people who had arrived at the campsite yesterday though, I wondered what we were supposed to do – pee and poo around the tents and caravans??!!! Who knows, involving the police may have changed things for the better for future visitors to this campsite.

I tiptoed away as discreetly as I could with my fully laden bike and bright yellow panniers, chuckling with relief and at the absurdity of it all as I pedalled back uphill into the town and straight to the local boulangerie for the all-important pain au chocolat and baguette for lunch.

It was a cloudy and sticky morning. I seemed to be climbing forever upwards, which was by now really starting to get to me. Mentally, I had been fully prepared for climbs in the Alpine and other mountainous regions. I was now in north-eastern France which I thought was flat or flatter. It demonstrates how important mental preparation and acceptance is. I was not prepared or accepting of this terrain at all. I was behaving as if the hills had suddenly appeared for my inconvenience. Childish, I know, but I thought best to get it out of my system and then I could carry on enjoying the trip.

In true "be careful what you wish for" fashion, I heard the first rumbles of thunder and saw the first flashes of lightening as I approached the summit of my long climb. Heavy sigh. Just what I needed. Much as I longed for a storm to clear the air, I didn't want it whilst I was actually cycling! Storms usually appear much later in the day, please stick to your usual schedule! There is a great photo on the blog of a severe rainstorm in the distance that soon engulfed me.

Waterproofs were donned and then removed. It was a better option to get wet with fresh rain water than sweat, it was simply too hot for waterproofs. I kept the overshoes on to protect my cycling shoes, though, as they can take ages to dry.

This being northern France, you can see for miles in front of you and all I could see were endless ups and downs, ups and downs. The chevrons on my map confirmed this wasn't an illusion. My knees were hurting, I wanted flat, flat, flat. I wanted to just pedal easily along after all my hard work in the mountains. I'd been looking forward to loosening off my legs as I reached this part of the country. Some of the gears on my bike were not fully functioning either but I hadn't come across a bike shop that was open yet in this cycling mad nation.

Perhaps the terrain was flatter after this bit, I thought as I tried to boost my flagging spirits. I stopped to eat my pain au chocolat, but even that didn't seem to help today. Oh dear, this was a serious Grump!

As I approached Laon after just 20 miles, I gave myself the option to stop if there was a campsite. There was! Excellent! Laon was a large town with shops that were even open, my luck was changing!

7 frustrating miles later and now considerably out of town, I found the "local" campsite. It couldn't have been further in the middle of nowhere, even down a long track that was over a mile long. I don't mind this at all but please, please, sell some basic supplies at the campsite if this is the case.

The "welcome" at reception did not improve the situation. A young man and woman were lounging around, smoking and drinking. I thought they were guests but they were apparently "looking after" the place. There was a small shop but they couldn't be bothered to open it. In fact, I discovered the next morning there was also a small bar but they had hidden the sign for that so that no-one disturbed their very important chatter. They didn't even want to take any money! They said they would do that tomorrow morning. I stressed I wanted to be off by 8am and really wanted to pay now. They refused and said they would definitely be here by 8am in the morning. They were here now…. I was truly perplexed.

I located the best out of a choice of dreadful pitches – more rocky, hard ground suited to the motorhome and caravan market. People don't seem to camp at campsites anymore. My tent pegs were really suffering and becoming very bent. I simply couldn't get all the tent pegs in here, adding further to my deepening frustration.

The rain came down in stair-rods just after I'd got the tent up. I dived into the tent, my panniers still outside. They are fully waterproof so it didn't really matter. I started to laugh at this point, dispelling some tension. At least I had got the tent up before the rain arrived. It was still so hot and unbearably sticky.

The facilities in the shower block were plentiful and would have been lovely had they been cleaned. The couple on reception needed to be sacked. This was not a well run or cared for campsite. I hadn't been to any campsite at all whereby the facilities were dirty. I assured myself it wasn't the end of the world and the shower water was beautifully hot, which improved my mood a smidgen.

I went back to reception to try to pay again but this was refused again. Determined to make them at least get up from lazing around, I asked if I could buy something from the ice-cream freezer that was stood right next to them. It didn't matter that I didn't actually want anything, I was motivated more by vexation with this couple. Luckily, they had a Magnum lolly, which I love, so I went away happy. I'd forced them to move and got something yummy out of it!

I settled down to do some more route planning, a more constructive activity. How could I find flat terrain as quickly as possible? That became my new over-riding goal. At least when climbing in the mountains, the spectacular views are completely worth it and keep you going. The achievement of reaching the top is fantastic. These hills were just debilitating. The scenery didn't change, there were no facilities or people and the road just seemed to go on and on and on (and on). And now it was raining to add to the fun.

By the evening, I was starting to feel much better and The Grump was losing power. I settled down to cook a nice pasta dish with the fresh food I'd bought in Aldi this morning. I had decided I would allow myself to stay in a hotel one night this week as a treat. That had been a considerable boost to my spirits. This tour wasn't supposed to be an ordeal, it was meant to be an enjoyable experience. If a night at a hotel would help, that's what I needed to do. Assuming I could find one in the villages and hamlets with no people……..

I'd also been in touch with cycling friends back home, arranging to meet them at Boroughbridge when I was back in the UK next week so we could all cycle back together. A welcoming committee to escort me home! I was delighted I had something so wonderful to look forward to upon my return to the UK.

It was time to settle down and let go of today. I was happy I'd managed to laugh at myself and I was happy to wave goodbye to The Grump as I drifted off to sleep.

Chapter 39 – Tuesday 21st August 2012: Cycling from Laon to Sancourt

There seemed to be a lot of activity at the campsite as I started to get ready this morning. What was going on? As soon as I walked to the shower block, I realised what was happening – the majority of people were scarpering before 8am to avoid having to pay! I didn't blame them, it was all the couple who were running the campsite deserved.

As I sat down to enjoy my breakfast, I realised the milk smelt funny and was starting to pour in big chunks. Ugh, it had gone off in the humidity! I had already filled my large bowl with a mix of cereals, dried and fresh fruit. I put it carefully to one side knowing that the little camp shop sold milk. If they refused to sell me any, I would smash the door down to get it. Nothing gets in the way of me and my breakfast!

I packed everything up and took my fully laden bike and myself to sit outside reception to wait for the couple. More motorhomes and caravans were fleeing the site. I was probably bonkers for still planning to pay.

Amazingly, true to their word, the couple did appear, admittedly with bleary eyes, dishevelled hair and looking half dressed, at 8am. They had clearly just this second got up. The chap then tried to charge me for a car, caravan, 4 people… Hang on, hang on, hang on. I was dressed in cycle kit and had a fully laden bicycle. He had seen me arrive wearing exactly the same cycle kit and on exactly the same fully laden bicycle yesterday. Seriously, what planet was this guy on?

We eventually got everything sorted and paid up and I was also allowed to buy some milk. I demolished my breakfast and, feeling completely relieved to leave this place, I set off for my next day of cycling adventure.

I'd seen a sign for the place I needed to head for today whilst cycling through Laon yesterday and made this my starting point. I was delighted I had done that. As soon as I picked up the route I needed, I cycled straight past a large Carrefour supermarket. Excellent! I happily stocked up on supplies.

Leaving the town, I was soon back pedalling through countryside. However, today was different. Usually, the roads were almost completely empty. Today, I seemed to be on a main artery to somewhere and there wasn't much room for traffic to overtake. I was being buffeted as heavy lorries swept past. I needed to get off this road swiftly.

I pored over my map and decided to deviate a short way further along this road. What a comfort to be back onto quiet roads and hear the birds sing again! Inevitably, this meant very up and down terrain with short and steep climbs and descents. I was, however, cycling through what felt to be an enchanted forest. I don't think I'd have been at all surprised if a fairy or goblin had peeked out from behind a tree!

I cycled through a delightful village called St Gobain and stopped when I saw a small café with a few tables and chairs outside. I wasn't missing the opportunity of a cuppa or mingling with real people again! It felt like normal life again with normal people going about their normal business in the local shops and banks. I drank my tea in the shade and chuckled when I shivered and goosebumps appeared. The temperature showed 27 degrees outside and I was shivering! I guess it was quite a dip in temperature compared to previous days.

My picnic lunch was on a bench overlooking a pretty square in Sinceny. I seemed hungrier than usual – obviously the "cold"!

I found it comical to cycle into a town called Ham mid-afternoon. What a great town this must be for vegetarians! I found a lovely looking small hotel, ablaze with a mass of vibrant and colourful flowers. I decided to stay here for the night assuming they had any vacancies.

Oh, it was shut. For heaven's sake, France, what is wrong with you?! When does anyone ever work in this country?

The next town was Peronne, 25 kilometres away. I usually liked to try wrapping up the cycling for the day by this time mid-afternoon, and I'd already cycled nearly 46 miles in hilly terrain. Sigh. I needed to pick myself back up and prepare for the next 25 kilometres of cycling. Off I went, pretending to feel strong and look alive.

I screeched to a halt a short distance away – there was a sign for a chambre d'hote, the French for bed and breakfast. It was in the middle of nowhere and it was on a farm. Please, please, please have a free room.

They did have a room, yippee!! Even better, they had a kitchen I could use to could cook my own evening meal. I'd had visions of setting up the Trangia outside on the pavement in the absence of anywhere else to cook. Plus using their facilities would save a bit more fuel in my rapidly diminishing gas canister.

I loved my little room. It had everything I needed including an en-suite – what luxury! The shower was truly fabulous and much needed. I got lots of clothes washed in the sink and they even had a spot to hang and dry them in the bathroom. How thoughtful.

I was so excited about using a real cooker and a real kettle this evening! It was such a novelty to stand up and cook rather than be sat on the grass, chopping vegetables and cooking on my ever-reliable Trangia. There was a dining room and lounge for guests adjacent to the kitchen. I discovered that a number of guests stay here all week every week for work, hence the facilities for cooking evening meals and the ability to chill out in the lounge, basically as if you were in your own home.

A huge bonus was being able to fully recharge my phone. I would normally collect all my texts and emails as well as write and send the blog from campsite shower blocks, which was the only place with plug sockets. You can only stand there for so long carrying out these activities whilst the phone is charging. Using the internet and emails really eats up the battery so my phone was usually operating on half battery or less. I kept it switched off during the day. I could usually tolerate standing in the shower block with the phone for around 45 minutes. Obviously, you couldn't just leave the phone charging and carry on with other things in case someone stole it. But here, in my lovely bedroom, I could. What bliss!

I was able to fully spread out my maps across the bed as well. I couldn't manage this in the tent, it was too small! I could clearly see my route to Calais and knew I would be very proud of myself for cycling all the way from the other side of Switzerland to Calais via lots of mountains and hills. Admittedly, I wasn't enjoying the hills in this part of France. The uphills were just a slog, the scenery remained unchanging and the downhills were not sufficient to make up for the climbs in the way that mountain descents are. It became my mission to find the flat part of northern France!

Chapter 40 – Wednesday 22nd August 2012: Cycling from Sancourt to Authieule

I was glad I hadn't been sleeping in the tent last night, the wind whipped up into a frenzy and the rain poured. It woke me a few times in my bedroom. My broken tent pole hadn't yet been tested in windy conditions. I was hoping it wouldn't have to be.

Knowing continental breakfasts can be quite small, I took my Weetabix and sultanas down to the breakfast room and was able to use their fresh, chilled milk straight from the fridge, another lovely bonus to being here. They had provided some gorgeous apple juice, 2 good sized bread rolls each with plenty of butter, marmalade and jam plus a mini pain au chocolat and a mini pain aux raisins. I felt ready to take on anything after that little lot!

I'd also had a very enjoyable conversation with one of the other guests, a girl from Belgium who spoke perfect English. She was very outdoorsy and sporty and therefore very interested in my trip. She was clearly a smart cookie doing some kind of bio-engineering work for the enormous agricultural factories I was frequently cycling past in this region. She did tell me what she did in English but it went straight over my head! It was so nice to have a proper conversation in my mother tongue again rather than my continuing stilted attempts in French. My spoken French had improved enormously over these last few weeks, which I was delighted about. My life on the road would have otherwise been quite silent if I couldn't converse with anyone at all.

I set off on a high; well rested, well fed and with clean clothes. I have to admit that the day became quite a grind again unfortunately. I love cycling and cycle touring so much, I wasn't sure why I wasn't enjoying it as much anymore. The terrain and scenery didn't help. The villages I was passing through were not very picturesque or inspiring anymore. In fact, they reminded me of the red-brick suburbs of Manchester, just on a smaller scale. It didn't surprise me that the town of Peronne that I cycled through this morning was twinned with Blackburn!

From the Swiss Alps all the way through to the Champagne region, the villages had been so beautiful with great character, personality and heart. The scenery had been awe-inspiring. I was now simply grinding out the miles to reach Calais. Having remembered cycling around northern France previously as completely flat, the climbs seemed annoying and pointless with no joyous descents. Worst of all, I could see for miles ahead and felt utterly dispirited seeing the forthcoming drags.

I was also cycling into a persistent headwind today. In the mountains, you can be quite protected from the wind and at least you can get out of it for short spells as you twist and weave your way up. In this region, I was heading in one direction only all day. Any cyclist knows how soul-sapping headwinds can be not to mention how much hard work.

This is where I needed to dig deep and keep myself entertained and focused. I counted down the miles to my campsite tonight. It had looked very pretty when I looked it up on my phone. I knew they had some kind of café/restaurant so I could treat myself to a meal out. Who knows, maybe they would even offer my elusive omelette, chips and salad on their menu! I sang songs in my head and smiled as much as possible. Apparently the simple act of smiling is meant to make you feel better and I have to say it worked! I recounted all my happy and amazing experiences from the tour so far, of which there were many. I thought of all the incredible support and encouragement I had received from everyone back home as well as everyone on the road, at campsites, at cafes, etc. I thought of how I would never take our 24/7 supermarkets for granted again and I planned to have the best-stocked fridge, fruit bowl and cupboards when I returned home! I couldn't wait to do a proper food shop and not have to worry about whether I could buy something based on its size, weight and ability to stay fresh in the heat. I would also without doubt cherish the humble fridge – this tour had taught me in a way that nothing else could what a tremendous invention this was. I appreciated and understood what life must have been like before fridges.

This helped me easily eat up all 47 miles to my campsite in Authieule. I'd made it and in good spirits!

There was a small patch of grass (yes, real grass!) for those camping in tents, the rest of the site was inevitably motorhomes and caravans in addition to permanent mobile homes. It was a very nice little site situated on a steep slope. The welcome was warm and friendly, the shower block was spotlessly clean with fabulous hot and powerful showers. Again, it was in the middle of a very small village with absolutely no facilities. I was glad they had a little restaurant as I was still trying to use my final gas canister as sparingly as possible. Being able to cook in a kitchen last night had been a great help.

The campsite menu was very basic and all meals were of the ready-made variety straight from the freezer. No omelettes. No matter, they fortunately had a vegetarian option. It was a four-cheese pasty and, given it wasn't very large, I asked for this with chips and lots of bread to fill up and asked if they had anything fresh to go with it at all. They said they had tomatoes so I ordered as many of those as possible as well. A lovely glass of chilled white wine also helped. Heaven!

There wasn't any indoor space, only a few tables and chairs set up outside for eating and drinking. The wind was still keen and had a bit of a bite to it. I had to go back to get my fleece to stay warm whilst everyone else, of course, remained in vest tops and shorts. I'm such a wimp!

Admittedly, it wasn't the best meal of the trip but I certainly appreciated it. I had plenty of fresh fruit and yoghurt back at the tent, which made a very nice dessert, along with a few biscuits and my ever-gorgeous mug of green tea.

The thought of reaching the coast either tomorrow or the day after was hugely uplifting. I knew it would give me a tremendous sense of achievement. I planned to get to the coast and then cycle the rest of the way alongisde the sea all the way to Calais. I'm usually in mountains and inland and therefore the sea would make an agreeable and satisfying change. I bet there would be chocolate crepes on offer in seaside resorts also! The weather forecast was sunny for the next few days and stormy again at the weekend. I couldn't help but laugh at the irony. France was just like Britain – the weather was generally lovely during the week when the majority of people are at work and then deteriorated in time for the weekend!

Chapter 41 – Thursday 23rd August 2012: Cycling from Authieule to Verton, near Berck

The temperature had definitely dipped. I slept in my silk liner as well as my sleeping bag last night. It is much easier to sleep when it is cooler and I love nestling down into my sleeping bag, which often feels like sinking into a fluffy cloud.

Today was a considerably better one for me. The cycling seemed easier, the hills were starting to flatten out (hurrah!) and the headwind didn't pick up until this afternoon.

I also managed to get my tyres pumped up today – double hurrah! From Authieule, it was only a few miles into the town of Doullens where EVERY shop seemed to be open. Will wonders never cease?! My first priority was the local café with its great ambience. I was unusually cold this morning so a hot chocolate was top of the list. That warmed the cockles! And then I returned to the bike shop I'd cycled past to see if they would very kindly pump my tyres up. I had my hand-pump but that was really for emergencies. I needed a good, solid, proper pump to keep the tyres firm for the rest of the tour. The shop owner kindly obliged and there was no charge. I love the French! I also stocked up on food provisions in this lovely town.

I was humming along to myself as I happily cycled through the countryside and alongside freshly hay-baled fields under blue skies, sunshine and cotton wool clouds. The temperature was more comfortable in the 20s. My windproof gilet, my staple item of cycle clothing that is rarely off my back, finally made a re-appearance after all these weeks of super-hot temperatures. The 20s felt so much cooler. If I found this cool, how would I cope being back in Yorkshire next week?!! The temperatures were not very high there at this point in time. I comforted myself in the knowledge that I was still carrying my full Winter kit should it be needed over the August Bank Holiday in the UK, a time of traditionally dreadful weather.

When hunger struck at lunchtime, I sat on a grass verge to eat my picnic, overlooking all the fields, listening to the birds singing and thoroughly enjoying my life on the road. A series of gunshots were suddenly fired, breaking my reverie. "My goodness, mind my bike tyres" was my first thought. It had taken me hundreds of miles and a number of closed bike shops to get those babies pumped up, I didn't need some farmer and a stray bullet destroying that. I then broke into helpless laughter wondering why on earth my bicycle tyres were apparently more of a priority than my own life!

Sobering up, I hoped and assumed it was a farmer who was shooting. I'm not sure what they were shooting at, but they were uncomfortably close. I decided a swift departure was the best, and most peaceful, course of action. It was not many weeks later that a British family and a passing French cyclist were tragically shot dead in a tranquil beauty spot near Lake Annecy, close to where I had been a short while ago.

Whilst researching potential campsites for today, I had read in one of the reviews that a number of campsites on the coast of north-eastern France no longer accepted tents. Heavens. whatever next? They shouldn't be allowed to call themselves campsites then, should they? How bizarre. My experiences in recent days were of campsites that mostly catered for motorhomes and caravans resulting in very poor ground for tents. It had been a relief to be heading back into an area with a plethora of campsites but now there was the slight doubt and concern that I wouldn't be able to, well, camp there. I wouldn't know until I tried and I hadn't been turned away from anywhere so far.

As a result of this knowledge, I dived into the first campsite I saw without cycling the extra handful of kilometres to the coast. However, the reception was closed. There was a notice directing me to the house opposite if reception was closed. There was no response at the house. Another notice gave me a phone number to call if no-one was around at all. It went straight to answerphone. The notice on the door stated that reception was only open from 10am until 12pm daily. What a tough life it must be working two hours per day in France!

I continued onto the next campsite. I had plenty of time to spare and plenty of energy left in the tank. I was simply concerned I might not be able to get in at these campsites.

I was successful at the campsite in Verton. This, again, was more of a holiday camp and it was absolutely huge with staff whizzing around on golf buggies to get about. They looked great fun! They did have a field full of tents, which was great to see. Fellow campers! Best of all was the huge map of Europe covering an entire wall in the reception area. This was the moment when I could physically see how far I'd cycled across two countries and my eyes welled up with pride and amazement. I wanted to shout to everyone "look what I've done!". I managed to restrain myself and calmly checked in like a normal person!

I located a sunny spot to pitch the tent with somewhere nearby to lock the bike up. Having got everything set up, I went in search of the shower block. I'd had to buy a token for the shower. Everyone knows how much I love those! All the showers cubicles were locked so I waited a short while. I realised I had heard no running water from any of the showers, in fact I had heard no movement at all. I tentatively knocked on the doors to which there was no response. The doors were all locked. How odd.

I went to reception to ask. They called a member of staff, who promptly arrived on a golf buggy to whisk me away to another shower block. Another hurrah for today, zooming along in the golf buggy was excellent fun! Apparently, most of the showers on the site were not working (wow, they're really on top of things here) so this guy took me to the disabled shower (how bad did I look?!). That shower did not need a token, grrr! All was forgiven as a long, hot shower washed away the day's grime and sweat and I emerged a fresher, cleaner and nicer smelling version of my cycling self.

The campsite won more brownie points with a very lovely glass of dry white wine for a mere 1 euro 50. I would miss France! To put this in context, a cup of tea was generally costing between 2 euros 30 and 3 euros.

I was back to camp cooking this evening. In Doullens earlier in the day, I'd spotted a packet of nice looking vegetable risotto, the key enticement being the "2 minutes to cook" emblazoned across the packaging. Sold to the lady with the diminishing fuel supply! It was advertised as suitable for 2 people, which obviously made it the perfect size for one hungry cyclist, and I added my own freshly chopped veg as well. It was absolutely delicious.

There was a wonderful and lively holiday camp atmosphere at this site and I enjoyed feeling a part of it as I relaxed by my tent. I was only a very short distance from the sea and would be cycling along the coast until I reached my final destination of Calais. I had decided to have a couple of short days to make my way up the coast rather than 1 unnecessarily long day. I would make Calais by Saturday, giving me a day to chill out on Sunday before catching the Bike Bus early on Monday morning. I was very pleased with the progress I had made and with these proposed timings, all being well. I had built in a bit of spare time should it be needed. And the train was still an option if something went wrong at this point with the bike, for example. I always have a Plan B up my sleeve!

Chapter 42 – Friday 24th August 2012: Cycling from Verton to Equihen Plage

I was up and away before most of the holiday camp even stirred this morning. I love having the mornings to myself.

It was only 33 miles of mostly easy cycling today. I was in a much busier part of the country but the French were as organised as the Swiss where cycling facilities were concerned. Good wide cycle paths ran alongside the main roads with a hefty verge safely segregating you from the traffic. The roads were not too busy, certainly not compared with England.

Etaples was my first stop this morning, a vibrant market town spilling over with people. It was nice to see so much life after several days that had seemed devoid of it. Perhaps this is where everyone from the villages I'd been cycling through actually came.

As I knew it was a short day, I was happy to take some time and stroll around, buying some fruit and veg from the local market stalls and taking my pain au chocolat to eat in the busy local café. Again, I felt very weird consuming something in a café that I'd bought elsewhere. However, most patrons at this establishment were doing the same.

I was just about running out of cereal and needed to buy some more for my remaining few days. I popped into the supermarket and found it a bit depressing to see a huge aisle dedicated to mostly chocolate and sugary cereals. This rubbish is what we are feeding our children? No wonder there are so many bad tempers. It was a challenge to find a small box of healthy muesli that would see me through my last few mornings before I returned home.

As lunchtime approached, I deviated from my route and headed straight for the sea. I wanted the novelty and luxury of a picnic on the beach in this gorgeous sunshine. The weather forecast had predicted rain. If it was en route, it was certainly holding off well. I was once again cycling under picture perfect blue skies and pleasantly warm sunshine.

On a day like this in the UK, the beaches would have been packed and you wouldn't have been able to see the sand for people. In Hardelot Plage, I pretty much had this vast expanse of white sandy beach to myself. There had clearly been quite a bit of building work in recent years and, whatever Hardelot Plage had been, it now had smart new apartment blocks overlooking the sea. There were almost no cars on the roads, the car parks were empty and only the odd roller-skater and family strolled by as I sat eating my picnic on one of the many vacant benches. A couple of families stopped to talk to me, seeing the fully laden bike propped up on the bench next to me. I received more "bravos" for my efforts now that I was just one day away from Calais.

It was hard to pull myself away from this spot and continue cycling. It was so peaceful and picturesque. I felt thoroughly content here. I was basking in fabulous warm sunshine.

Reluctantly, I moved on. I stuck to the quieter coast roads for the rest of the day. They were inevitably more hilly and twisted and turned more, however it added more interest to the ride. It was exquisitely pretty with some really cute villages. What a pleasant change after the last few days of soulless red brick towns!

As I cycled towards Equihen Plage, I caught my first glimpse of England! There they were, the white cliffs of Dover. I hadn't been expecting that at all and I felt strangely emotional. There was my home country. I was so close to home. So near and yet so far. I suddenly felt immensely homesick. I couldn't wait to see everyone again. The few days I had left suddenly felt like a long time. And yet this conflicted with the emotion of not wanting the tour to be over.

Time to pull myself together and find the campsite here. I reluctantly headed down the long steep hill into Equihen Plage. I was sincerely hoping the campsite wasn't located at the top. I'd taken a good look around and the signs were definitely pointing down into the town.

I followed the signs down and through the town and almost right out the other side. The campsite was very attractive and well kept and had definitely been worth locating. It was situated on top of a steep hill (aren't they always) resulting in everyone having a fantastic view of the sea. Again, I inhabited the only tent. The site provided a patch of grass to pitch on and I did my best to find the flattest bit, it was on quite a slope. Much as I wanted to pitch with the door facing out towards the sea, any breeze felt to be coming from the sea. I needed to pitch with my door facing up the hill. For the first time in what seemed like an eternity, my tent pegs went easily into the ground and the tent felt fully stable.

The showers at this site earned the joint top prize with Masevaux in the Vosges. They were absolutely perfect, scrupulously clean and both the temperature and power were spot on. It was the first time I had come across showers operated by a card. It worked, that was the important thing. I could have stayed under that shower all day!

The facilities were plentiful and everything was superbly clean and cared for. They provided washing machines and tumble dryers. I enthusiastically bought a token for the washing machine but they didn't sell any powder. Reluctantly, I had to give the token back. I didn't want to risk putting shampoo in their washing machine and damage it. I knew I'd be home soon, it would just have been nice to have cleaner smelling clothes for the bike bus journey back.

I set off for a meander along the seafront and back into the town. The sky was starting to look distinctly more grey than blue. Perhaps the rain was finally making its way over. I was carrying my waterproof jacket just in case.

I enjoyed another super cheap glass of very tasty dry white wine whilst sitting writing my diary. This café/bar was in the middle of a residential estate. Again, there was very little life although I assumed most people were out at work.

As it clouded over further and became ominously dark, I decided to head back. I'd got some nearly dry washing hanging out and I didn't want to risk those getting a soaking.

Luckily, I timed it all really well. The rain hung off until I was not only back at the tent but also after I'd cooked my evening meal! The winds had started to whip up and I was very grateful I'd pitched the tent in the direction I had. I could sit in the porch, chopping and cooking vegetables, fully protected from the increasing gusts. I kept looking up at the broken tent pole. It didn't look to be having any difficulties with the wind, in fact it looked more robust with the sleeve so firmly welded over it.

The rain started as I was finishing eating. It wasn't too heavy and I opted to wait and let it pass. I left my pots and pans outside to let the rain start cleaning them – efficiency!

It became apparent that the rain had no intention of stopping. In fact, it was becoming heavier and more persistent. Time to don all the waterproofs and make a dash for it down to the shower block. I winced as I covered their pristine white-tiled floor with my mucky footprints. I was quite shocked at the turn in the weather, despite the forecast. The calm, warm and pleasant Summer's day of earlier had transformed into a very wet and windy evening.

I sat in the tent reading my Kindle, a little nervous about the broken tent pole in such conditions. The wind and the rain seemed to be worsening all the time. I couldn't do much about it. I'd double-checked the tent pegs were in as far as they could be and the tent was stable and coping well with the gusts. I would have to place trust in the tent. I had pitched it as well as I could and the fencing just behind the tent protected me.

I would need to try to get a good night's sleep and hope this had all passed by tomorrow morning.

Chapter 43 – Saturday 25th August 2012: Cycling from Equihen Plage to Calais

I didn't have my best night's sleep of the trip. The weather didn't help nor did the continuing concern regarding the broken tent pole. However, the biggest problem turned out to be one of the lights in the campsite shining directly onto me all night. Usually, lighting was much more subtle and campers were expected to use torches when walking around in the dark. Even my eyeshades couldn't block out the bright light entirely. It was a bit like sleeping in broad daylight.

The rain had stopped by the morning. The wind was still very strong and blustery. This would make riding along the coast interesting! My broken tent pole had held up admirably and my tent had fully protected me all night. I'd heard a family arrive in a car late at night and they had experienced real difficulty getting their large family tent up. They hadn't secured it properly and it had been flapping crazily all night. I'm sure that didn't help any of us sleep either.

The strength of the wind was actually quite scary as I walked the bike down the campsite to set off. I hadn't realised it was quite so brutal. I would need to be very careful whilst cycling today. My heart sank at the task ahead. This was going to be a very tough day and take every ounce of strength I had left. A headwind is bad enough but there wasn't just me getting in the way, there were my panniers as well. Time to dig deep again and keep my spirits up – this should be my last cycling day in France and I should reach Calais today.

Up the long and steep hill back onto the road I needed to be on. I seemed to be cycling OK. More than OK, in fact, had the wind suddenly stopped? It slowly dawned on me that something almost unprecedented in the world of cycle touring was taking place – I was benefiting from a very strong tailwind! Oh my goodness, this was going to be a GREAT day!

I was off! Flying along the D940 coast road, which, despite the roller coaster nature of this route, I would recommend to anyone. I'd almost lost faith in anything in northern France being particularly scenic but this was beautiful. The dark clouds scudding across the sky added to the drama and beauty of this wild coastline. I was also amazed and impressed to see very little building here, it was still raw and natural in many places. The bulk of the traffic was on the nearby autoroute (motorway) and I therefore frequently had the road to myself.

I cycled through many villages and areas with some great names, such as Dunes de Slack (named after the river Slack but still made me chuckle) and Ambleteuse, which I thought sounded really pretty.

I achieved my fastest speed ever today at 46mph!! That clearly shows the power of the tailwind behind me. I'd actually never experienced anything so fantastic, I was flying along, barely able to keep up with my pedals on some occasions! There were some switchbacks en route so the ride wasn't a complete doddle but it was much easier than I had originally anticipated.

One of the most enjoyable moments of today was cycling out of the huge urban sprawl of Bologne. This involved a long climb. I'd seen the climb from a distance and was mentally geared up for it. As it happened, I'm sure I didn't need to pedal up the hill, I was simply blown up! The wind was so strong, it was giving me almighty shoves up. The strength of the wind was actually quite scary, I'd never cycled in anything so strong. But I was just laughing uncontrollably, it was like being a kid again with some crazy uncle giving you enormous shoves up the hill! There were some people around and about so I pretended to pedal to make it look like it was me working hard to zoom up the hill so impressively quickly. I could have done that again and again, it was like a fun fairground ride!

I was at least staying warm with the wind firmly behind me. I also escaped the rain for much of the day although inevitably it arrived in style as I neared Calais. I had started my tour in bad weather, I would apparently finish it in bad weather. I was forever grateful that I had experienced mostly good weather in between, the storms mainly occurring at night.

I couldn't have been more saturated as I entered Calais. What a way to finish the tour! Dedicated cycle paths led me safely through this large conurbation. I needed to be on completely the other side of the town where I would be staying at the Camping Municipal, right alongside the beach and the port.

A large puddle formed around me as the rain ran off my clothes in the few moments it took to check in at the Calais campsite and obtain a detailed map of the town. I squelched off to find a camping spot, one that was as sheltered as possible in these gales. Groan, it was back to hard, rocky ground more suited to caravans and motorhomes. In fact, it was reminiscent of waste-ground, it was extremely poor. I had a real job trying to get my tent up. The wind was determined to pinch it from me. As I laid the tent down on the ground, I had all 4 panniers holding it down. I put one pannier inside the door and was glad I'd done that as the wind did succeed in ripping the material from under the other 3 panniers and the tent took to the sky. Fortunately, this one pannier inside was holding it down. I couldn't catch the tent until that gust of wind had gone. Others nearby were unhelpfully laughing and shaking their heads in disbelief at the strength of the wind. A hand from them would have been useful but never mind.

Trying to drive the tent pegs in was ridiculous. I had to attempt it time and time again, the ground was useless. I had some spare tent pegs with me and drove those in as well to secure the tent as much as possible. The tent was still flapping like crazy but I'd pulled it as taut as I possibly could and the pegs seemed to be holding. I looked around for some good rocks, bricks, anything heavy to anchor the tent further but there was nothing of use. Better ground would have made a considerable difference.

Erecting the tent had been harder than the 33 miles I'd cycled today! It was time to celebrate the end of my cycle tour. I donned full waterproof clothing and braved the elements for the short walk to the beachfront cafes.

The wind seemed to be picking up still further. Large blackboards advertising menus and specials outside the cafés had been slammed over. Outdoor tables and chairs had been secured. People were battling to walk in an upright position, all leaning into these ferocious gales.

I was able to ignore it all as I indulged in the most fabulous chocolate crepe and pot of tea of the trip. With so many people on the blog telling me I was amazing, I now finally felt that I'd achieved something amazing. Everyone's support had helped so much. I was deliriously happy. I couldn't wait to get home to share all my experiences with everyone and find out what they had been up to. At the same time, I also didn't want this to end. I changed my thinking and thought of it as an exciting new beginning instead. I was lucky to have created the opportunity to do this tour and had turned a negative – leaving a job that wasn't working out – into a real positive. I was very proud of myself for that.

Even better was I'd seen the ever-elusive omelette, chips and salad on the menu at this café! I would most certainly be returning here this evening! On a previous tour from Calais down to the Mediterranean, the only meal I was able to eat for two weeks was omelette, chips and salad and I swore I'd never eat it again. Now I couldn't wait!

Back at the campsite, 3 of my tent pegs had been ripped out by the wind. Fortunately, I found them all nearby and re-secured them as best I could in the useless ground. I was intensely concerned about the tent surviving this evening. I was worried about every tent pole, not just my broken one. By the time I had showered (the showers were only open between 4pm – 9pm and for a couple of hours in the morning), the front tent peg had been ripped out so the porch was fully exposed and the tent door was flapping crazily again.

The heaviest thing I could find to support weighing down the tent pegs were my water bottles filled with water. I used all three bottles and hoped for the best before heading out for dinner.

Whilst tucking into the omelette, chips and salad meal I'd been craving for so long and enjoying a celebratory glass of wine, I looked through all the papers for the bike bus collection point. I realised this was actually at completely the other side of Calais rather than right by the port where my campsite was situated. I thought I'd found the perfect spot! With the combination of the appalling weather, being in the wrong location, being in a celebratory mood – this was an early 40th birthday treat to myself after all – and, no doubt, the wine, I set about researching any reasonably priced hotels close to the bus pick up point. The Ibis Calais Car Ferry seemed to fit the bill and I booked myself in for the next day. Boy, did I feel good for doing that! A room with an en-suite would be the perfect way to relax and freshen up before an early morning start on Monday to join the European Bike Express home.

I stayed in the warm café and out of the vicious winds, for as long as possible before heading back to the tent. Fortunately, the tent pegs had stayed in although the wind was physically lifting the fully filled water bottles. I had never seen my tent bend and flex so much. Nervously, I got inside and tried to settle down. Similar to last night, I had a bright light shining straight onto my tent and face, which didn't help.

The winds had seemed to be easing but then as midnight approached they whipped up into an even greater frenzy. The gales were tearing at the tent, the pegs were being ripped out throughout the night and I continued to dash out and put them back in. The tent relies on the pegs to pull the walls taught otherwise they almost fully collapse around you. The front tent pegs were pulled out most frequently, despite the water bottle attempting to anchor them down, resulting in the tent door battering my face over and over again. There simply wasn't any good ground to put the pegs into. The noise from other tents flapping violently in the gales didn't help at all. I kept whipping my eyeshades off after every excessive blast of wind to check my tent was still standing. The deafening roar of the wind was not unlike that of a jumbo jet engine. I resigned myself to the fact that I wouldn't get any sleep tonight. It wasn't the end of the world, I didn't have to get up and go to work tomorrow.

What a way to finish the tour! I felt to be in the throes of a hurricane, such was the noise and ferocity of the winds. Well, it was making it memorable! The effects of the usual dreadful English bank holiday weather were certainly being felt in France!

Chapter 44 – Sunday 26th August 2012: Rest Day in Calais

I was so glad when morning dawned having been awake most of the night. My tent had somehow miraculously survived, even more incredible considering I had a broken tent pole. Other people's caravans and attached awnings were in varying states of disarray. I had now had 2 nights of very little sleep and I'd got an early start tomorrow morning to catch the Bike Bus. Although I felt groggy, I reminded myself I could catch up on sleep when I got home, I wasn't going straight back to work.

I ate breakfast in the tent with the tent walls billowing around me head. Thank goodness I hadn't had to endure similar conditions all tour. Hearing the ferries in the port, I sincerely hoped the winds would ease before our Channel crossing tomorrow.

After updating my diary and blog (my Mum was particularly anxious to know I'd survived the night), I wandered down to the beach and seafront. It was still ridiculously wild. Very few people were out and, those that were, were still struggling to stand up and walk properly in the blustery conditions.

A nearby café was open where I enjoyed a reviving hot pot of tea and a delicious pain au chocolat. I spent a good proportion of the morning here, relaxing whilst reading my Kindle, which was still impressively going strong. What an amazing battery life they have!

Heading back to the campsite, I packed everything into my panniers with great happiness and relief before making my way to the Ibis Car Ferry hotel, where I could check in from midday. My bike chain needed lots of attention after the rain and crud on the roads from yesterday. I spent a while working on this. My bike had looked after me, it was my turn to repay the favour. She worked effortlessly and like a dream afterwards.

The hotel was a good few miles away, outside of Calais town and its facilities. I had to walk a good chunk of it, too, as the main route to the hotel was closed to traffic for the Sunday market. There were too many people milling around to cycle through safely.

I was in high spirits as I reached my hotel and was shown my superbly clean and perfect room (near perfect; the addition of a kettle to make gallons of tea would have made it truly perfect). As soon as I'd unpacked, I set back out on foot with my map to find the exact location of where the bike bus would collect me the following morning. I was a little apprehensive as to what I would find as the pick up point was at a place called "Boozers car park". Oh dear! As it turned out, there was simply a motorboat showroom here and a flower shop; no alcohol or alcoholics in sight! My only slight concern was it being situated in a remote location, albeit near the motorway and main roads, and I would be here on my own early in the morning. There was also nowhere to shelter if the weather was bad and no facilities, e.g. toilets or cafes, if the bus was late. There may well be others turning up to join the bike bus as well, I reasoned. And I'd been assured there would be updates provided should the bus be delayed so I shouldn't be standing there for too long. In fact, I'd already received notification that the bus was delayed by 2 hours 15 minutes on the way from England to France due to ferry crossing delays caused by the dangerous winds.

Relieved that I knew exactly where I needed to be in the morning and how to get there, I headed back for a cuppa in the small but sweet hotel garden before then walking back into Calais town. My poor feet! I was used to cycling not walking lots of miles!

Although still windy, the gales were finally starting to ease considerably. The sun had come out, the people had come out, the flowers had come back out; Calais looked a completely different town. I was keen to head to the beach to see what it actually looked like in sunshine. There would be the added benefit of treating myself to another delicious chocolate crepe! It seemed to taste even better than yesterday. Perhaps the café was really looking after me given I was now a regular after multiple visits in the last 24 hours!

It was an absolute luxury and indulgence to shower, change into the cleanest clothes I had and relax over a 3-course dinner in the hotel restaurant in the evening. No worrying about getting grass stains whilst sat cooking on the trangia outdoors. I could sit on a real chair to eat! I was able to treat myself to some lovely fresh food: a large mixed salad with a tangy dressing and fresh French bread for starters; an asparagus, pea and broccoli risotto for the main course and, to complete my very piggy day, some exquisite vanilla and chocolate ice cream. All enjoyed with a large glass of chilled dry white wine, of course. The waitress and I conversed in French throughout, even though her English was excellent. I heard her speaking fluently to a number of English guests. Again, not one English person so much as attempted a "hello" or "thank you" in French even though I was certain they would know what the words were. Please, anyone reading this, just have a go! I probably made a complete idiot of myself trying to pronounce various words but the French people love you for trying and will help you. It's all part of the fun and joy of travelling.

Before settling down to sleep in my extremely comfy bed with its soft and fluffy pillows and duvet, I checked with the bike bus again. They had made up a bit of time on their route down to northern Spain. It was feasible they could make up all the time by tomorrow morning so we agreed I would call the bus as soon as I got up in the morning. If they were still delayed by a couple of hours, at least I could stay in the comfort and safety of the hotel.

I didn't think I would sleep well knowing I had a 5am start, however I was soon in the land of nod and making up for my last two sleepless nights.

Chapter 45 – Monday 27th August 2012: Travelling by European Bike Express

I felt wide awake the second my alarm woke me up at 5am. I immediately phoned the bike bus to find out if they were still delayed and what their expected time of arrival in Calais was. There was no response so I left a voicemail. I was awake now so jumped into the deliciously hot shower to freshen up.

Feeling strangely nauseous, I headed to the hotel restaurant. The hotel brochure advertised a limited breakfast from 4am and then a full breakfast from 6.30am. I would be gone before 6.30am. However, the chap on reception said nothing had yet been set up for breakfast. Not to worry, I still had muesli and milk back in my room. I felt much better after eating.

I called the bike bus a further 3 times, twice in quick succession in case they couldn't immediately get to the phone. I left another voicemail. I then also sent a text followed by an email. I really did not want to head to Boozers car park at 6am if the bus was not going to arrive for another 2 hours. There was no response to any of my communications.

Feeling disappointed in their sudden and unexpected lack of service, I reluctantly decided to set off. I couldn't risk missing the bus if they had made up time. I just couldn't understand why there was no response. I didn't have an issue with them being late at all, these things happen, I just had an issue at the complete and utter lack of communication. It would have made such a positive difference.

As I carried my panniers to reception to check out, I discovered the chap on reception had fully opened the restaurant for breakfast. He hadn't known which room I was from when I'd popped down nearly an hour ago to let me know I could now eat breakfast. I felt so touched he'd done that just for me and then terrible because I needed to leave. Well, I thought I needed to leave. I explained my predicament to him as best I could in French. He wasn't happy at me waiting alone at Boozers car park either and attempted to call the bike bus himself from the hotel phone. He did not receive a response either.

I thanked him for his exceptional level of service and headed out on the bike. Thankfully, it was a stunning morning and very quiet at that hour. The skies were clear and the winds had eased to a light breeze. I arrived at Boozers car park at 7am, unhooked all my panniers and turned the handlebars round, as instructed. It would then take a couple of minutes to get both my bike onto their trailer at the back, the panniers into the luggage area and me onto the bus.

Apparently incapable of simply sitting and doing nothing, I sat painting my toenails to look a bit more girlie as the sun started to rise. It actually felt quite special at that time in the morning. I was extremely grateful the weather wasn't bad as there was simply nowhere to shelter. I also managed to help a Spanish truck driver, who was lost, find his way to the port with a mix of pigeon French from both of us and lots of finger pointing on my detailed map of Calais. What a wonderful feeling to be able to help someone from another country who spoke another language!

At just before 7.30am, I finally received a text message from the bike bus simply stating their ETA into Calais was 9.15am. It was a shame it had taken them so long to respond but I could at least now head back to the hotel for a feast of a breakfast.

I received a very warm welcome back to the hotel, they all seemed to know the predicament from this morning and were very happy to see me. I loved this hotel! And what a feast the breakfast was: fruit juice, lots of choice of cereals with chilled milk (a rarity on this tour and therefore a luxury this morning), fresh fruit and my favourite fruit compotes, yoghurts, breads, jams and marmalades, crepes, cakes, teas, coffees, I was in my element. I had to laugh at the children who came into the dining area, running around in awe at the choices available to them (especially the cake!).

Fully replete and adoring the hotel even more than before, I once again cycled back to Boozers car park to wait for the bike bus. I was clearly the only one being collected from Calais.

What a sight it was when it arrived! A double decker coach with a large bike trailer behind. Loading the bike, panniers and me was very efficient and took impressively less than a couple of minutes. The interior of the bus did not smell great with lots of touring cyclists just waking up in the morning after a night of sleeping on the bus!

It was, of course, just a short ride to the port of Calais. We had to wait on the bus to find out which ferry we could get on and, fortunately, we were able to squeeze onto the very next one leaving for England.

It was great to stretch my legs and wander around the ferry on the short crossing to Dover, which took around an hour. Despite the rather significant amount I'd already eaten this morning, I still managed a large mug of tea and a berry muffin en route. My excuse is keeping the food and drink intake up helps me a great deal with motion sickness, both on the ferry and for the bus journey ahead.

Fortunately, I was sat at the very front of the coach, having explained to European Bike Express that I do get travel sick. There was as much tea and coffee as you wanted available on the bus for a very reasonable price throughout the journey. I was initially sat next to a lovely guy who was a teacher. He was originally from South Africa and had moved to the UK a number of years ago. He had just completed his very first cycle tour. He had just decided to have a go and didn't even have a bike so he'd borrowed one from a friend! Crazily, he'd tackled a route across the Pyrenees for his first trip. Luckily, he was fit and had thoroughly enjoyed it. He was simply determined to have his own bike next time. He had decided he wanted to build his own bike, in fact. That would be his project in the winter months. I was impressed. He then informed me he was getting off the bus a stop earlier than planned because he needed a nearby bike shop to mend a puncture before he could cycle home…. He would have a steep learning curve if he wanted to build his own bike and yet was currently unable to mend a puncture!

He left the bus shortly after arriving in Dover, giving me lots of space to stretch out at the front for the rest of the day. Inevitably, it started raining shortly after arriving in the UK. It was Bank Holiday Monday after all! As we worked our way up the country, the countryside looked pretty sodden and sorry for itself. There wasn't the usual colour and vibrancy in people's gardens. It had obviously been as wet and miserable as everyone had been telling me on the blog.

I found travelling on the bike bus very comfortable and an extremely convenient way of travelling with the bike. I happily chatted to the other cyclists on the bus, everyone swapping stories on where they'd toured and where they recommended. Basic food and drink was available whenever you wanted it. I was delighted that they had one of my all time favourite dishes – macaroni cheese! This I ate for a lunch followed by a cheese and tomato toastie later in the afternoon. There were also a couple of stops at service stations en route. It was great to get some fresh air and move around. I was beyond shocked at how cold it felt in the UK compared to France. The others were laughing at my golf sized goosegumps!

We arrived into my stopping point in Boroughbridge around 3 hours later than planned. I'd contacted the campsite to let them know and asked them to keep some milk for me. What hadn't dawned on me at all is that it would be dark at 8pm when I arrived. It was getting dark around 9-9.30pm in France. Of course that was the equivalent of 8-8.30pm in the UK with the one hour time difference.

There was only me leaving the bus at Boroughbridge. Most people had already left the bus at others points in the country and just three people remained on for the final drop off point. My bike, panniers and me were deposited on the pavement in the rain and in the dark. I'd already got my waterproofs on but I wasn't in cycling gear. The streetlights were not particularly effective. I struggled to see properly putting the screws back in to secure the handlebars back into place. Wet hands didn't help a great deal. I talked myself through it calmly to carry out the task as quickly and efficiently as I could. It was easy to pop the panniers back on, thankfully.

Now, time to find the campsite. I'd researched where it was before embarking on the tour and confidently set off. I put my head-torch on….oh. The battery had chosen this moment to die. Brilliant. I had a good back light and 3 helmet lights flashing away plus I was in my hi-viz waterproof cycling jacket. I knew cars could see me. I hoped I would have streetlights all the way to the campsite otherwise I would have difficulty seeing the road without my head-torch.

I cycled along as quickly as I could and followed my map and directions as best I could in the dim light. I pedalled and pedalled, quite out of breath in the unfamiliar cold air. I was cycling much faster than my usual pace in my desire to find the campsite as quickly as possible. Just as I thought I should be reaching the campsite, to my horror, I turned up back at the place I'd set off from. Oh heck!

I'd been up since 4am UK time, on a ferry and a bus all day, now it was dark and raining, my headtorch wasn't working at the worst time and I seemed to be really disorientated and clearly not thinking straight. STOP!!

I phoned the campsite again and they gave me the clearest instructions on how to find the site. I set off again, pedalling more calmly and steadily this time. I was now cycling on unlit roads, feeling rather unnerved without my headtorch and hitting multiple potholes as a result. I had to stop and call the campsite again for directions. I was truly baffled. I'd just managed to cycle across two European countries and yet I was hopelessly lost in the small town of Boroughbridge!

Thankfully, the campsite owners were extremely calm and patient and talked me through every step of the way. Perhaps they were used to semi-hysterical solo female cycle tourers. They also stood outside the site in the rain, flashing a torch to guide me in. Thank goodness for such kind-hearted, lovely people in the world!

Now the really fun part – putting the tent up in the dark! My front helmet light provided a small amount of visibility, the hardest bit being working out which of the two poles went where whilst avoiding snapping the broken tent pole further. At least I had the comfort of knowing I had pitched the tent almost every day for the last 6 weeks so should be very experienced at this! Again, I talked myself methodically through every step and, to my delight and amazement, had the tent up in almost no time at all. And the inside had stayed dry! The poles had been slippery in the rain but I'd got there. The tent pegs had gone into the ground smoothly and effortlessly. I was extremely proud of myself!

Once inside the tent, I could finally put my tent light on for some visibility. I heard the gentle patter of the rain on the tent fabric and felt relaxed and cosy. I was once again camping on soft and sweet smelling grass, such absolute bliss! I organised everything in my tent in the way I had perfected over the weeks, enabling me to settle down to sleep in complete comfort, shattered from the journey and rather stressful time since leaving the bike bus. I couldn't wait to meet the others and cycle home with them tomorrow.

Chapter 46 – Tuesday 28th August 2012: Cycling from Boroughbridge to Home!

Seriously, was I back in England? Wasn't that SUN warming up my tent?!

I was still on French time so had woken early, around 6am. The birds were chirping away, the sun was coming up and the sweet smell of the grass was still so noticeable and welcome. I opened the tent door to be greeted by blue skies and fluffy white clouds. Hurrah, I'd brought the European weather back with me! Everyone would be pleased!

There was no rush, I wasn't meeting the Welcoming Committee until around 11am. They had to cycle to Boroughbridge first. The milk had stayed perfectly cold overnight (yes, I was back in the UK then!) and I enjoyed the very last of my muesli. Even better, I still had sufficient gas in my canister to enjoy a brew, what utter heaven!

Whilst enjoying my cuppa in the warm morning sunshine, watching the rest of the campsite stir into life, I was astonished to see another solo female cycle-camper walking towards me with a big grin. We were both delighted to see another of our kind! I had not met a single other female cycle-camper travelling alone in all these weeks and, come to think of it, nor on any tour I'd done in the Yorkshire Dales.

This lady was called Karen and she had been cycle touring for many years. She confessed that she had only ever met one other solo female cycle-camper on all her travels and that was the famous Josie Dew. I've read most of Josie Dew's books and she's one of my cycling heroes.

Karen and I swapped stories. She was doing a slightly unconventional tour from Mansfield to Sunderland. She was so enamoured with my tour and asked me lots of questions, all the questions I'd had myself before setting out and those that I have sought to answer in this book – concerns over transporting the bike and panniers to and from Europe, arranging a route, camping without pre-booking, managing in a foreign language and cycling alone (others seem more concerned about this than either Karen or I). We were chatting for around 45 minutes, it was a wonderful way to spend part of the morning. I could have spent much more time with Karen and her stories.

Before she left, she declared that I'd inspired her to attempt her first tour to Europe next year when it would also be a big birthday for her. I was absolutely thrilled – to inspire others either to try cycle touring or to stretch their cycle touring horizons is the best outcome I could ever hope for. I sincerely hope my adventures have inspired others reading this book to give cycle touring a go. Try a weekend away, you'll never look back! When Karen returned from her tour, she did read my blog and also wrote some comments on there. I was jumping up and down with excitement! Karen, if you're reading this, I look forward very much to hearing or reading all about your first solo cycle tour in Europe in 2013. You'll love it!

Buzzing with happiness and energy, I packed my tent away for the last time on this trip and headed to the café where I was meeting the others. Incredibly, we all arrived at the same time. There were lots of congratulations, back slapping, hugs and, of course, attempts at picking up my fully laden bike. It didn't have any food in the panniers any more, no gas canisters and I'd only got one water bottle filled rather than all three so it was quite a bit lighter than usual, although many still wondered how I'd cycled up mountain cols carrying such weight. Very slowly, I replied!

I was so thrilled to see everyone again. They were mostly glad I was back safely. As I've repeatedly said, I experience such kindness from others whilst out on the road, whether in this country or abroad. I think everyone thinks of me as their daughter/granddaughter/sister and therefore look after me. I genuinely have never had concerns about my own safety and seek to reassure everyone that this is the case. They themselves wouldn't hesitate to help anyone on the road, why would anyone else be different. I know there can always be that one person who ruins everything but you can't spend your life worrying about that, you'd never do anything otherwise. Plus I was travelling in civilised western European countries, I was hardly in the back of beyond!

I indulged in my first traditional UK cyclists lunch of beans on toast at the cafe. And I was able to drink gallons of tea rather than being restricted to the one small cup you receive on the continent. One thing I never understand over there is why they bring you a small cup of tea or sometimes a small cup of hot water with a teabag on the saucer but then a large jug of milk?

Ramsay told me he'd done his first long weekend cycle tour, inspired by my tour and also the Tour de France and the Olympics. Awesome! That was the 2nd person inspired by cycle touring in one day! I was very proud of him for giving it a go and also enjoying it, despite the wet weather he encountered en route to the Lake District.

In a jovial mood, we all set off to cycle back home, chatting nineteen to the dozen in the surprising and welcome sunshine. We must have looked a slightly peculiar group with mostly guys on lightweight road bikes and then me encumbered with multiple panniers and bags. The chaps did offer to take some of the panniers off me, however I was used to the weight now and was perfectly balanced. I just requested they go a bit slower than usual so I could keep up.

We stopped en route for afternoon tea in Knaresborough. They knew how much I loved and needed my tea! Unfortunately, we experienced an injury here. Brian, who has never come off his bike before, hit a pothole and somersaulted off his bike (we unanimously graded him 10 out of 10 for his impressive dismount). A few days later, he discovered he'd cracked a few ribs in the process. This didn't stop him cycling, of course. The hospital had ordered him to rest. His rest was cycling! I'm sorry you became injured, Brian, whilst escorting me safely home. On a positive note, I finally got the opportunity to use my new multi-tool getting his handlebars safely back into place after his crash!

I thought I'd feel really sad cycling up my road, locking my bike up in the garage and walking back into my flat after all these weeks. As it happened, I didn't have time to feel sad. One of my neighbours had just parked up and wanted to know everything about the trip. Another neighbour knocked on the door when I was already half undressed and about to jump in the shower, he was keen to know how I'd got on. I didn't realise at the time that I had several flies and midges stuck to my sweaty face, I must have looked great! I was in a rush because I'd arranged to see some friends up the road before they left for a fortnight's holiday at 6am the next day and I was already late.

In fact, I didn't get the chance to shop for some basic supplies or even unpack any of my panniers that evening. I was home quite late and desperately, desperately needed to go to bed and indulge in a luxurious long, deep sleep. I'd earned it!

Chapter 47 – The life changing impact of extended cycle tours!

Well, I did it, I'd made it! I'd cycled nearly 1,400 miles (over 2,000km) all the way from the far east of Switzerland via mountains and hills, dales and valleys to the north coast of France and in all weathers whilst carrying my home and on my own. What an extraordinary adventure! And, can you believe it, NO PUNCTURES or any form of breakdown of my bike – what a workhorse and true touring superstar. I can therefore heartily recommend the Ridgeback World Voyage!

When I set out on this trip, it was partly to find out if I could do it and if I would enjoy solo cycle touring. I didn't know if I could cycle up Alpine cols on a fully laden bike. I didn't know if I could plot my own route. I didn't know if you could just turn up at campsites and get straight in. I didn't know how I would cope with difficulties thrown at me. I didn't know how easy or difficult it would be to travel on public transport with my fully laden bike. I now know I can do all those things and much more and all whilst having the most fantastic time.

And now to answer another big question – what do you do and how do you cope when you return from such a fabulous adventure? How do you re-integrate back into "normal life"?

Firstly, I'd been very sensible and had organised and booked activities and appointments in for the first few days and weeks I was back. This was absolutely the best thing to do to keep me busy and my mind occupied. It felt a bit surreal being home after such an incredible adventure. Life felt tremendously easy in comparison, with every modern convenience in my home and a supermarket less than 100 yards away. It was nice to be back in my own bed. And I loved being back amongst family and friends. I was keen to avoid becoming an absolute bore talking non-stop about the tour however people seemed genuinely interested, asking me lots of questions. I still have people now, several months later, saying what a wonderful thing to have done and achieved, how they admire me and how brave I was to do this. I didn't feel brave at all, cycle touring is what I love most in the world and I simply took every day as it came. These memories, the support, friendliness and kindness of those I met on the road and the lessons I learnt on tour will stay with me forever.

So what did I learn from the tour? That I'm capable, I'm resourceful, I can get through whatever I need to creatively and with a sense of humour (and a mug of tea!) and I want to continue carrying this courage and confidence with me in everyday life. The tour has opened up a lot of possibilities in my mind, not just for touring, but also for life itself. And I also learned what incredible family and friends I have who supported me the whole way. Even they wanted me to continue touring, they were missing their daily blog updates!

Did I feel sad to be home? In some ways, yes. However, this wasn't going to be my last trip ever. I also knew it was up to me to bring the life, energy, heart, soul, spirit, new experiences and adventures from the tour into my everyday life. I knew finding my next job would be an adventure in itself given we were in the depths of the deepest recession in a generation!

What I didn't realise at first was just how much I'd changed as a result of the tour. Do bear in mind I was also just turning 40 and possibly having a mid-life crisis! I knew I would struggle going back into a 9-5 job again, no matter how hard I tried to think positively about it. This just wasn't the right way forward for me at this point in time.

Despite being someone who had always craved security, I decided to do something I had only ever dared to dream about in the past. I set up my own business. I now run an imaginatively named business services consultancy called Andi Lonnen Business Services (I'm an accountant, I'm not a creative marketing type!) providing part-time finance director services to small and growing local businesses and I also provide financial and business training, coaching and mentoring around the UK. Previously, my fulfilment at work had always been in making a positive contribution and helping to grow and develop both businesses and the people within them. By providing part-time services to several different companies at the same time, I can now help many more businesses achieve their goals rather than just the one company I am usually employed in.

Having carried out all sorts of personally scary activities in my life, such as skydiving, bungee jumping and white-water canoeing, setting up in business is hands-down the most terrifying thing I've ever done! But it is easily the most exciting, challenging and extraordinary time of my life also.

Whatever happens next, I'll always be immensely proud of myself for having the courage to give it a go. That applies to both the cycle tour and to setting up in business. I almost feel like a 5 year old child again: hugely excited on a daily basis, on a great voyage of discovery every day and then so terrified, all I want to do is hide behind my Mum's skirt!! I have an enormous, new-found respect for all those who start their own businesses!

So, life has changed in the most unexpected and fantastic way in the last few months. I sometimes wonder if I'm dreaming, it still feels quite surreal (the long hours keep it real!). And this is all because of a cycle tour! You have been warned if you are planning an extended trip away!

The final question I am always asked: where will you go on your next tour?

Who knows? All I do know is my trusty tourer, tent, Trangia and I can't wait to get back out on the road, exploring new and exciting places, meeting new people and enjoying the freedom that cycle touring brings.

One thing's for sure, I can't wait to get planning again…..over a nice cup of tea!

Blog address including photos of the tour: http://andilonnen1.blogspot.co.uk

Swiss-French Cycle Camping Tour Kit List

HOME & SLEEPING ARRANGEMENTS
- Tent & footprint (groundsheet)
- Tent light
- Self inflating sleeping mat
- Thermarest sleeve to convert sleeping mat into chair
- Down sleeping bag
- Thermarest pillow
- Silk sleeping liner
- Fluffy bed socks!
- Beanie microfleece hat
- Eyeshades & earplugs

BIKE, BAGS & BITS
- Ridgeback World Voyage steel touring bike
- Ortlieb rear panniers
- Ortlieb front panniers
- Ortlieb rack pack (to carry tent & sleeping gear)
- Ortlieb handlebar bag incl map case
- Cycle computer
- Pump (attached to bike)
- 3 water bottles
- 2 x cycle locks
- Lights:
    - rear light (already attached)
    - head-torch (strap to handlebar bag if needed)
    - 3 helmet lights: 1 front, 2 rear
- Tools & Repairs:
    - 3 spare inner tubes
    - Puncture patches
    - Tyre levers
    - Multi-tool allen keys
    - Multi-tool
    - Small bottle oil
    - Chain link & chain link extractor tool
    - Disposable gloves
- Emergency foil blanket
- Yellow straps to strap items onto racks
- Hand-wipes

COOKING & EATING EQUIPMENT
- Trangia and screw top gas canisters
- Matches
- Pan & frying pan (doubles as pan lid)
- Mini kettle
- Spork & knife set, teaspoon

- Titanium mug
- Cheery bright pink indestructible beaker (used as beaker, wine glass, dessert pot and bucket for bailing out floodwater)
- Awesome collapsible bowl & plate (base of both double as chopping boards)
- Penknife (complete with wood saw....)
- Dishcloth/sponge/washing up brush
- Small teatowel
- Mini leakproof bottle washing up liquid
- Zip lock bags to carry t-bags, sultanas, couscous, pasta, etc.
- Mini leakproof bottle olive oil

CYCLE GEAR
- Helmet
- Cap (essential for so many weather conditions)
- Eyewear with interchangeable lenses – clear & sunglasses
- Gore waterproof Paclite
- 2 x short sleeved cycle tops
- 1 x long sleeved cycle cardi
- 1 x cycling vest top
- 1 x long sleeved thermal top
- Windproof gilet
- 2 x sports bras
- 2 pairs cycle shorts
- Waterproof RainLegs
- Waterproof overshoes
- Cycle gloves – fingerless and full-length Winter gloves for mountains
- 2 x neck buffs
- Fleece ear-warmers (for mountains)
- Cycle shoes
- 3 pairs black ankle socks
- 2 small carrier bags with hair bobbles to put over gloves if severe mountain weather

EVENING CLOTHES
- 2 x convertible North Face trousers (convert to ¾ length and shorts)
- White long sleeved Zoca top
- 2 x Rohan T-shirts
- 1 x Rohan vest-top
- Fleece sweater
- Fleece body-warmer
- Undies
- Silk travel pyjamas
- Lightweight pac-a-mac waterproof jacket with hood
- Navy blue waterproof overtrousers
- Walking sandals
- Flip flops for shower block

SHOWER, TOILETRIES & MEDICATION
- Black string bag to carry items to and from shower
- Travel towel
- Shampoo
- Facial wash
- Toothbrush & small toothpaste

- Small deodorant
- Small sweet smelling body lotion
- Mini talc
- Mini bottle lavender oil
- Mini hairbrush, comb, travel mirror
- Mascara, lipgloss
- Earrings, watch
- Small waterproof eye make up remover pads
- Small pot facial moisturiser
- Mini tube handcream
- Medication/first aid:
    - Inhalers & asthma tablets
    - Tramadol painkillers
    - Paracetamol, Ibuprofen
    - Mini tube Savlon cream
    - Plasters
    - Chafe-Ease cream
- Sun-cream
- Baby-wipes
- Mini bottle hand gel

ESSENTIAL TRAVEL DOCUMENTS
- Passport
- Travel tickets
- Cash in relevant currency
- Pre-loaded travel card
- Credit card

EVERYTHING ELSE!
- Toilet roll
- iPod
- Kindle
- Blackberry (doubled as camera) & charger
- Tissues
- Notebook & pen to write diary
- Maps, guidebooks

OTHER IMPORTANT NOTES:
- Carry emergency contact details form in sealed envelope in handlebar bag

Made in the USA
Middletown, DE
27 October 2014